A Blueprint for 21st Century Leadership

_________________________________, Leader.

About the Blueprint for 21st Century Leadership

Leadership is not for the faint-hearted, nor is it a career that is suited to everyone. Many managers believe themselves to be leaders, but get stuck in the operational weeds; they fail to think strategically, or lack a collaborative mindset, or maybe the humility required to succeed as a leader, inspiring others to deliver the vision.

Perhaps you have been selected to attend our leadership program because you have been judged to have leadership potential. Your company has great expectations of you - during the program, and afterwards.

Or perhaps you have purchased this Blueprint workbook because you are ambitious, and keen to make the right impact as a leader within your organization.

Are you ready to become a 21st Century Leader?

Why this workbook?

There are many books available on the subject of leadership, so how is this one different? Some titles are heavily academic, based on extensive research, filled with conceptual models. Others are written by time-served leaders who are experts in their fields. This Blueprint for 21st Century Leadership hits the sweet spot between academic rigor and business relevance. As consultants teaching in an academic environment, we are up to speed on current academic thinking, but are also in the privileged position of advising on, observing and benchmarking operational and leadership best practice within global organizations from a consultancy perspective. It serves as a guide to new and existing leaders, and contains a selection of key slides, notes, handouts and references from the comprehensive leadership development program provided by Catapult Consulting Ltd, along with plenty of space for your own notes and self-reflection. As a training aid, it is a world away from loose-leaf pages which become lost or tatty, and it will serve as an easily-identifiable learning artifact for you to read, complete, inwardly digest, and revisit in the future. It contains myriad tools, techniques, checklists and models to sharpen your thinking and refine your practice.

Some organizations do little or nothing to help future leaders to raise their game. Or perhaps your organization has created an ethos of investing in the development of its people, shaping and refining organizational culture in a way that reaches across every level of the organization, or maybe you are just working it out for yourself.

As well as supporting clients across a range of sectors - manufacturing, defence, financial services, pharmaceutical, engineering and public sector - all over the world, author Claire Sutherland also manages to find time to work as a visiting lecturer at the highly respected Universities of Warwick, Aston, Kent, and Singapore Institute of Management where she lectures in leadership at Master's degree level to students from across the globe. Her research draws upon contemporary leadership theory, coupled with real-world organizational experience, and she has built an enviable reputation for her practical hands-on approach to leading and managing in 21st century organizations.

Catapult Consulting Ltd

- Founded in 2005
- Organisational development consultancy
- Specialists in building high performance organisations
- Clients include MoD, Ministry of Justice, AbCam, Alstom, Atlas Elektronik, Barclaycard, BUPA, HMRC, Hospira, IMI plc, Mastercard, National Grid, NATO, Quadient, Sainsbury, Severn Trent Water, United Nations, Visa
- Operating in UK, Europe, USA, South America and Asia
- Visiting lecturer at the Universities of Warwick, Aston, and Kent Business School
- Based in East Sussex and the Cotswolds
- www.catapultconsulting.co.uk

Catapult Consulting

Claire Sutherland MBA

Claire has been working in executive development for the past 30 years. First and foremost, she is a practitioner, who brings real organizational experience to the programs she designs and delivers. She founded Catapult Consulting Ltd in 2005. She delivers specific interventions in strategic alignment, emotionally intelligent leadership, executive coaching, communicating change and creating high performance culture.

She has an MBA from Aston University, is qualified in MBTI, FIRO-B and a range of other psychometric instruments. She has an advanced Diploma in business coaching, a certificate in Transactional Analysis, a Certificate in Sport Psychology, is an NLP practitioner, and a founder member of the Centre for Applied Positive Psychology. She is also a member of the Institute of Directors.

Check out our website to read about the work we do and some of our clients, and discover the many ways in which we can help you.

Contents:

INTRODUCTION

This Blueprint for 21st Century Leadership is a step-by-step guide which has been created to help you follow a logical sequence to leading and inspiring the people in your team, and to support the continuous development of a high-performance business culture. It provides you with tools, techniques and practical ideas to help you in your leadership practice, plus questions to get you thinking about how you can play your part in improving performance across your business.

Each section is carefully designed to guide your thinking and provide sequential advice on covering all elements of strategic leadership during challenging times.

Good leaders inspire and encourage their people to achieve the extraordinary, and most of us can recall a really good leader who has helped us to grow and develop our career. This is your chance to be that transformational leader who your people remember.

Ultimately, there is no substitute for practice, and your greatest learning will come from applying what you have read here and discussing it with your colleagues.

Leading people is one of the greatest privileges we have in our career. This book is about how you can **contribute** to the growth and development of the people in your team, and deliver the vision and mission of your organization, now and in the future.

Wherever you see this toolkit icon, this indicates that the model, checklist or structure is a highly relevant and proven business tool to help you lead your people to high performance. You can use the tools on a daily basis to raise your leadership game.

There are a lot of these toolkit icons throughout this book. That's because although the book is carefully researched and rooted in academic theory, it is written to be immediately relatable, relevant, and practical, and to help you to be the very best leader you can be.

In fact, you can get started on putting them into practice right away.

Part One: Why do YOU want to be a Leader?

Definitions of Leadership

There is no single definition of leadership, because there is no single all-encompassing style of leadership which is right for every situation. Indeed, leadership is rather contextual. The person who starts an organization and grows it from nothing to a multi-million-pound enterprise is possibly not the best person to lead through a business plateau, or indeed, a downturn. Healthy organizations play to the relative strengths of each of their leaders and work hard to ensure that the right person is at the helm at the right time. So, leadership may be less one long solo performance, and more a collection of key player and cameo roles, depending on the circumstances. With that in mind, you are invited to read through the different concepts, theories and models presented here and consider how you will tailor them to create your own bespoke leadership style.

Jack Welch, often-quoted head of GEC was once heard to say, “Everyone wants to be Jack Welch, and copy my style of leadership. Don’t. Work out your own style, and do that, instead.” Accordingly, much of the ground work of leadership is about self-awareness, flexibility, and a large helping of humility. There is no leadership without followers, and no followership without respect and trust. People won’t follow you just because you tell them that they should. They will follow you because you explain the big picture to them, sell them a compelling vision for the future, and invite their input in bringing it to life.

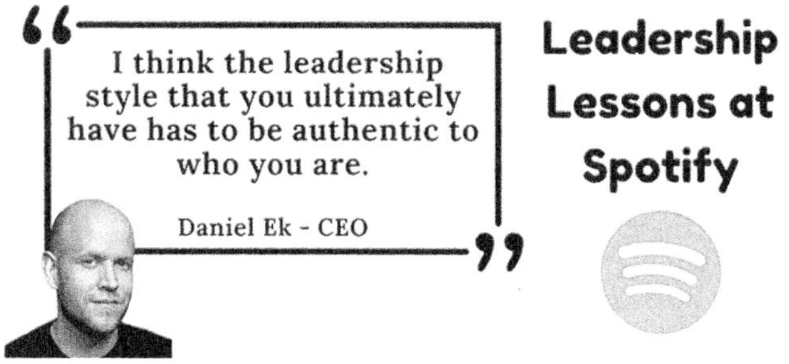

Whatever you have learned to date about leadership and management, park. There will always be new insights to integrate and to synthesize into an updated version of what 21st century leadership looks like.

Author Eric Hoffer observed, "In times of change, it is the learners who inherit the earth; while the learned find themselves beautifully equipped to deal with a world that no longer exists." Stay hungry, and forever be learning.

You, the Leader

An organization may enjoy state-of-the-art facilities, use leading-edge technology, operate with best practice policies and processes, but it is still your people who get the job done. As Simon Sinek said, "All your customers are people, all your suppliers are people, and all your employees are people. If you don't understand people, you don't understand business."

No surprise, then, that this leadership program focuses strongly on people - who they are, what drives them, and how to tailor your leadership style to get the best from each and every one of them.

But first, let's consider your own motives for leadership. Why do you want to be a leader? Is it the money? The status? The career advancement? Or is it because you're really passionate about helping people grow and ensuring that your business will thrive? When we lead others, we need to make sure that we are in the right mindset. A job in leadership may well pay more, but your work will shift from doing the job yourself to getting it done through other people.

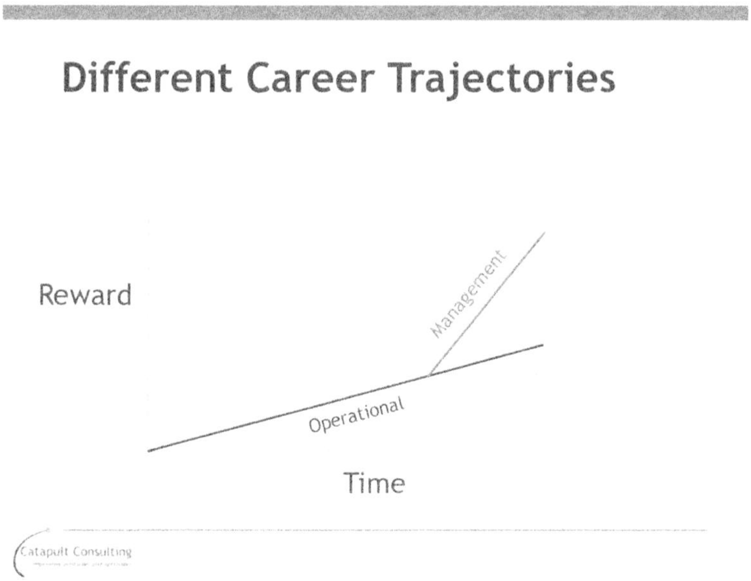

No doubt your salary will almost certainly increase faster if you pursue a career in management (and ultimately, leadership), but are you really suited to it? Many strong operational performers may be attracted to a career in leadership under the mistaken expectation that they will simply be doing more of the same kind of work, but at a higher level and for more money. What many don't factor in is that leadership is all about people: articulating a compelling vision for the future, setting inspiring goals, communicating important business messages so that people can understand how they contribute to the success of the organization, and all of this with one eye on the external marketplace so that you can lead business change quickly and effectively when needed.

The Role of the Manager:

- To manage people on a daily basis, regardless of when / where they work
- To set clear and compelling performance goals
- To link individual goals with strategic imperatives for greater relevance
- To measure progress against those goals
- To provide regular feedback on performance
- To make recommendations for improvement and development
- To follow the processes defined by HR, Finance and other departments
- To check in regularly with staff to help them focus, align and aspire to delivering the goals of the organization
- To plan the work
- To support the team to enable the work to happen

The Role of You, the Leader:

- To hold the vision, mission and values of the organization in the forefront of your mind at all times, using them to guide everything you do
- To decide on the best competitive strategy to accomplish you mission and deliver your vision for the future
- To communicate the vision, mission and strategy to every level within the organization
- To add value to the organization and to your colleagues
- To inspire your followers to do the right thing (even when you're not looking!)
- To role-model the behaviors and values you wish to see throughout your organization
- To set clear expectations for the evolution of the business, never allowing yourself or your colleagues to become complacent
- To keep on learning every day in order to remain relevant in a changing context
- To show up as the best version of yourself, every single day
- To grow a generation of new leaders

Many new leaders (and far too many time-served, experienced leaders) don't realise the extent of their responsibilities, and prefer to stay focused on operational tasks that they like and enjoy. But that's not what leadership is about.

Part One: WHO ARE YOU?

- Leadership in your organisation
- Different strokes: understanding personality
- Leader, know thyself
- Understanding strengths
- Leading on purpose
- Goals for personal effectiveness
- True North

Catapult Consulting
Improving attitudes and aptitudes

This is the structure of part one. You will see that it demands of you some self-reflection, and asks you to consider who you are, and who you are being when you come to work.

Self-awareness is the foundation stone for all personal and professional development. Without a clear understanding of why you are the way you are, you cannot become ready to polish your style and impact as a leader.

Inspirational Leaders

- Think of a leader who has inspired you. Use them as your role model.
- Identify what makes them so effective in their approach to communication
- What is it that they are saying or doing that you admire?
- How does their performance impact the audience?
- Discuss with a colleague and agree the behaviours that you would like to emulate

- Share your thoughts

What is Personality?

- A person's preferred style of behaviour
  - strongly influenced by social conditioning
- We are creatures of habit, and tend to behave predictably in certain situations...
- ..which means that we tend to be consistent over time
- If behaviour was predictable or reliable, there would be no point in measuring it
- One method of measuring personality is the Myers Briggs Type Indicator (MBTI)

Catapult Consulting
Improving attitudes and aptitudes

The MBTI test is based on research by Swiss psychologist Carl Jung (1875 - 1961). His research was developed by mother-and-daughter team Katherine Briggs and Isabelle Briggs-Myers into the MBTI test, which was initially used to assess women entering industrial work during and after WW2, to facilitate their finding work that was comfortable and to which they were best-suited.

Nearly 60 million people have completed the MBTI assessment around the globe, and it remains the most statistically reliable test of personality to this day. Businesses, educational institutions and government organizations worldwide use this test.

72% of the UK population agree with all 4 letters of their reported type. If your reported type and your best fit are not the same, there may be a number of reasons for this. The mood you were in, or the context and situation you were in when you completed the assessment (such as a job interview) may impact to some degree the way you completed the questionnaire. Similarly, cultural pressures (such as the organization your work for, your family and upbringing or the wider culture of your community) may have some influence your answers.

Myers Briggs Type Indicator is the registered trade mark of OPP Ltd. For more information, and to complete a full personality profile for yourself, please visit https://eu.themyersbriggs.com

How would you describe your own personality?

How would others describe your personality?

Is there a difference?

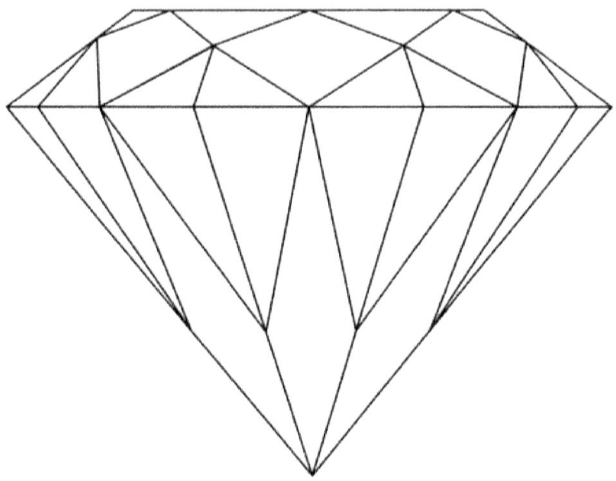

Personality is like a multi-faceted diamond, and different groups with whom you interact will see different facets in specific contexts, and may not even recognize the other facets so easily. Why is that, do you think?

Some people feel that they have to pretend to be someone else when they come to work, in order to fit in. This places a huge mental strain, and is very draining. Why do you think people feel the need to wear a mask at work?

Do you wear a mask to work? And if so, why is that?

What is the real, authentic version of you which sits at the core of all the different facets of your personality?

Myers-Briggs type indicator

What MBTI is:

- Measure of our dominant preferences for taking in information and making decisions
- May not be polarised clearly between scales
- So, you can be "a little of both"
- No profile is better or worse than another
- Helps explain our working style preferences
- Based on the theory of Carl Jung

Catapult Consulting

What it is not

What the MBTI isn't:

- A measure of abilities- it's not a test
- No right or wrong answers
- Not trying to put you into a 'box'- more a map to understand differences
- MBTI is an 'indicator'- you can agree or disagree

Catapult Consulting

How comfortable do you feel with being labelled as a 'type'?

How do you think understanding your own type - and that of others - could help with communication and leadership?

Can you see how useful it is to measure personality, using a respected and proven framework for understanding?

The MBTI test measures personality preferences across four different dichotomies, outlined over the next few pages.

Rabbit or Duck?

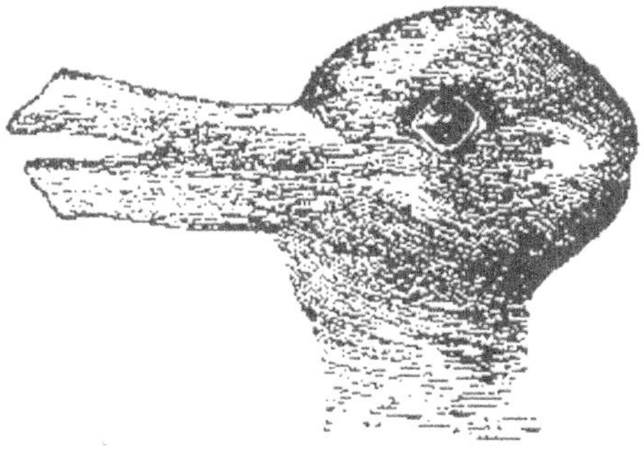

Catapult Consulting

Can you see both?

"There can be no peace until they renounce their Rabbit God and accept our Duck God."

Catapult Consulting

Most conflict arises from the inability to see the world from another perspective.

Understanding the different personalities of the people we live with and work with provides a deep insight into how our style is just one approach. Allowing other people to be who they are, and having the confidence to be who we really are, rather than trying to fit in, leads to a much more functional set of relationships.

You will probably find that much of the developmental criticism you have received in your life will probably have come from someone telling you that you need to be more like them.

What are the common themes to feedback you have received in the past from parents, teachers, friends, partners?

It is naïve to assume that our way is the only way. We can learn from people who are different to us, and they will likely be very strong in areas where we are weaker.

Introversion vs extraversion

KEYWORDS ASSOCIATED WITH EACH PREFERENCE

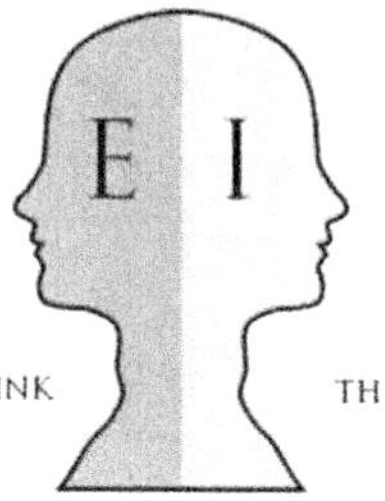

Catapult Consulting

Extraversion

Strengths

- Talk to people
- Let them know what's going on
- Include and motivate people
- Lively in a team

Weaknesses

- 'Wish I hadn't said that!'
- Don't always think things through properly
- May seem opinionated
- May not seem interested in other ideas

Catapult Consulting

Introversion

Strengths

- Think things through carefully
- A calming influence
- Communicate in a considered way, choosing their words

Weaknesses

- 'Wish I had spoken up!'
- Don't always speak up at the right moment
- May be seen as quiet, and not joining in

Catapult Consulting

Sources of energy: Introversion or Extraversion?

Which of the descriptions for introversion or extraversion sounds most familiar to you?

Where do you have the most difficulty relating to others?

In what way do you contribute at work, in terms of your extraversion or introversion?

How does your opposite 'type' complement your approach?

Sensing vs iNtuition

KEYWORDS ASSOCIATED WITH EACH PREFERENCE

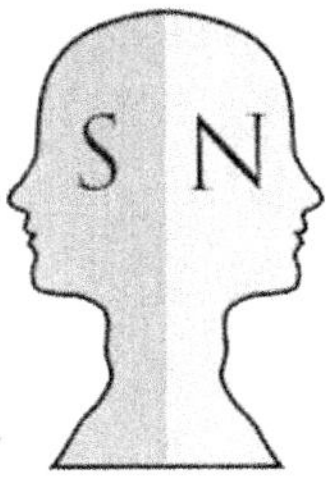

Sensing (S)	iNtuition (N)
FACTS	IDEAS
DOWN TO EARTH	DREAMS
PRACTICAL	THEORY
MAKE	CREATE
FIVE SENSES	IMAGINATION
EXPERIENCE	VISION
PAST AND PRESENT	FUTURE

Catapult Consulting

Sensing

- Strengths
  - Fact-based
  - Good at remembering specifics
  - Learns from past experience
  - Grounded in reality

- Weaknesses
  - May miss the 'big picture'
  - Could miss opportunities and possibilities
  - Lack of future focus
  - May get stuck in the detail

Catapult Consulting

iNtuition

- Strengths
  - Helicopter vision
  - Good at seeing patterns, links, themes and opportunities
  - Future-focused

- Weaknesses
  - Not so good at the detail
  - May ignore past experiences in favour of new ideas
  - May be a little impractical at times

Catapult Consulting

How do you process information: Sensing or iNtuition*?

Which of these descriptions sounds most familiar to you?

Where do you have the most difficulty relating to others?

How does your preferred approach to processing information - Sensing or iNtuition - help you at work?

How does your opposite 'type' complement your approach?

* iNtuition is written this way (rather than 'Intuition') because we use the initial letters to describe your Myers Briggs 'type'. We already used 'I' for Introversion, so we simply use the next letter along.

Thinking vs Feeling

Keywords associated with each preference

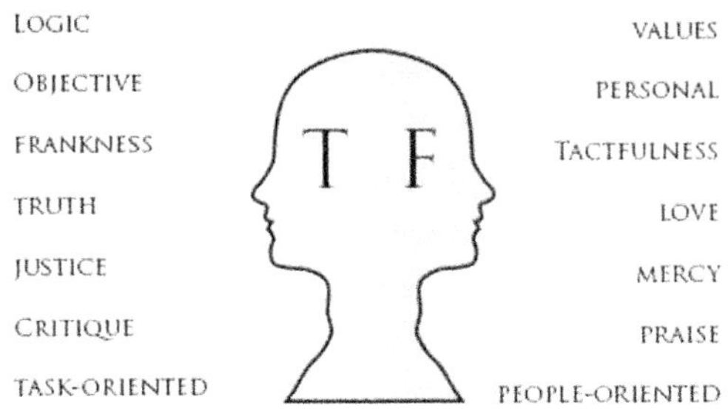

Catapult Consulting

Thinking

Strengths:

- Logical processing
- Good problem solvers
- Gets the job done

Weaknesses:

- May be too focussed on process
- May "ride rough-shod" over other people
- May be "tone deaf" in their communication

Catapult Consulting

Feeling

Strengths:

- Works to create harmony between people
- Focus on common ground
- Praises spontaneously

Weaknesses:

- May lack task focus
- May be considered to be "soft and fluffy"
- Decisions may lack logical analysis

Catapult Consulting

What do you rely on for decision-making - Thinking or Feeling?

Which of these descriptions sounds most familiar to you?

Where do you have the most difficulty relating to others?

In what way do you contribute at work, in terms of your Thinking or Feeling-based decisions?

How does your opposite 'type' complement your approach?

Judging vs Perceiving

KEYWORDS ASSOCIATED
WITH EACH PREFERENCE

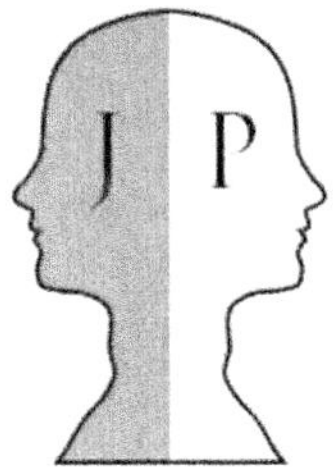

CLOSURE	OPENNESS
DECISION	OPTIONS
SCHEDULED	SPONTANEOUS
ORGANIZED	DISORGANIZED
PLAN	EXPERIENCE
CONTROL	FLEXIBLE
NOW	LATER

Catapult Consulting

Judging

Strengths

- Planned and organised
- Manages time well, avoiding last minute stress
- Set times for work and play

Strengths

- May be too rigid in their plans
- May resist last minute change, or find it stressful

Catapult Consulting

Perceiving

- **Strengths**
  - Flexible and open to new information
  - Thrives on last-minute time pressure
  - Spontaneous and adaptable

- **Weaknesses**
  - Disorganised
  - Last minute panic
  - Untidy desk, no plan!

Catapult Consulting

How do you organise your time - Judging or Perceiving?

Which of these descriptions sounds most familiar to you?

Where do you have the most difficulty relating to others?

In what way do you contribute at work, in terms of your Judging or Perceiving approach to organization?

How does your opposite ‘type’ complement your approach?

ISTJ ISTJs are considered, pragmatic and dependable. They are meticulous coordinators of people and events. Thoroughly in command of all necessary facts, they are adept at making plans real and workable. ISTJs value consistency and make decisions in a logical and reasonable manner. They are traditional and loyal, and like to operate in a structured and efficient environment.	**ISFJ** ISFJs are methodical, friendly and conscientious. They are gentle and unassuming organisers and protectors of tradition, working conscientiously to nurture those they care about. Good listeners and keen observers of people, situations and places, they have a rich understanding of the intricacies of the lives of those around them. They value loyalty and like to operate in a harmonious, supportive environment.	**INFJ** INFJs are caring and imaginative. They think deeply about the links between work and people, and build complex conceptual frameworks to explain these connections. Charming and perceptive, they see positive potential in everything. The INFJ working style is calm and organised. They prefer to operate in an environment that is ethical and developmental and which provides meaning to those working in it.	**INTJ** INTJs are independent, with a clear inner vision of the way the world should be. They enjoy intellectual challenge, thrive on debating theoretical ideas and concepts and value competence. Most enjoy finding new systems and approaches that will help to achieve a long-range vision. INTJs prefer to work in an environment that is structured logically, with room for autonomy and independence.
ISTP ISTPs are realistic and analytical. Quietly spoken and self-contained, they dislike rules and regulations, preferring the flexibility to respond and adapt to situations. ISTPs are keen observers of people and things. Their ability to make logical sense of their observations typically results in realistic and efficient solutions. They are at their best in a practical and task-focussed environment that provides autonomy.	**ISFP** ISFPs are sensitive, friendly and kind. Guided by their deeply-held people-centred values, the wellbeing of others is very important to them and they will work tirelessly to keep their obligations. ISFPs like to live in and for the moment, with the freedom to respond, rather than any requirement to stick to routine tasks. They value intimacy, and prefer to work in a co-operative environment of compatible colleagues.	**INFP** INFPs are committed, faithful and empathic. They are interested in developing a vision for the future and are guided in this by their deep, personal values, which they use as a compass to guide them through possibilities. Although quietly spoken, they can be inspirational and are passionate about any cause to which they are committed. They enjoy working with others who share similar values and ideals.	**INTP** INTPs are easy-going, with an intellectually curious approach to life. They are independent and form their own opinions, which tend to be theoretical and strategic. INTPs are natural sceptics, seeing logical inconsistencies. This can lead to new insights and inventive solutions. They value objectivity and prefer a task-focussed work environment, in which all can make an independent contribution with their own expertise.
ESTP ESTPs are energetic, resilient and adventurous. They are attuned to the here and now. They are resourceful and particularly enjoy responding to a crisis or emergency in a practical way. ESTPs like to live life to the full, and typically enjoy a wider range of physical activities. They value the freedom to think and act spontaneously, and do their best work in a fast-paced and results-orientated environment.	**ESFP** ESFPs are vivacious, energetic, spontaneous, sociable and fun-loving. They learn best through personal experience shared with others. They thrive on variety and are attuned both to practical realities and the needs of other people. ESFPs are loyal and enjoy being able to help. They like to be where the action is, at the centre of an energetic, harmonious team that allows a flexible response to each individual's needs.	**ENFP** ENFPs are fun loving and enthusiastic optimists. They are innovative problem-solvers who enjoy developing visions of the future through sharing their thoughts and ideas with others. They are in tune with others' emotional needs and use this insight to create possibilities for growth and development. Valuing relationships, they do their best work in a flexible and harmonious environment full of opportunity.	**ENTP** ENTPs are flexible, insightful and innovative. They look for the new and leading-edge ideas and are excited by novel concepts, which they use to develop strategic visions for change. They see myriad future possibilities and like to keep options open as long as possible. ENTPs value autonomy and competence, and prefer environments that offer variety and complexity to keep them challenged.
ESTJ ESTJs are efficient, achievement-orientated organisers. They like to take charge, to 'plan the work and work the plan', performing tasks diligently, methodically and with a sense of urgency. They are honest and direct, valuing an objective and logical analysis of the facts. ESTJs are quite traditional, and prefer to work in organizations where there is clarity in the structure, systems and processes needed to get the job done.	**ESFJ** ESFJs are sociable and caring harmonisers. They place great value on people, believing that everyone is unique and that each individual should be acknowledged, valued and supported. They are keen observers of people and situations, respecting tradition and established ways. ESFJs like to be at the centre of things, taking responsibility for bringing warmth, harmony, security and fun into the lives of those around them.	**ENFJ** ENFJs are gregarious and passionate facilitators. They place great value on harmony in interpersonal relationships and are seen as warm, caring, compassionate and demonstrative. They have an optimistic vision of the future, pursuing those ideas that will maximise the benefit for all concerned. ENFJs are conscientious, and prefer to work in a structured environment where clear expectations allow everybody to fulfil their potential.	**ENTJ** ENTJs are logical, decisive, energetic and business-like. They like to take charge, seeking excitement from being centrally involved in planning and overseeing activities. They want to be respected for their initiative and competence in addressing complex problems. They make strategic and long-term plans, and follow these through with determination. ENTJs have a clear task focus, bringing structure and efficiency to any environment.

Mapping Your Leadership Team

ISTJ	ISFJ	INFJ	INTJ
ISTP	ISFP	INFP	INTP
ESTP	ESFP	ENFP	ENTP
ESTJ	ESFJ	ENFJ	ENTJ

What can you learn about your leadership team, based on the distribution of personality 'types'?

Heterogeneous Teams Outperform Homogeneous Teams

Leaders and managers alike often fall into the trap of recruiting others who think the same as they do. That can only lead to Groupthink. A Finance team may be staffed by people with analytical minds, focused on the detail, whereas Marketing is often populated by visionary inventors, who look to the future. A company led by a Marketing CEO may be so focused on the future that the company runs out of money in the short term. A company led by a Financial CEO may miss future opportunities because they are playing it too safe in the present. It is the combination of perspectives that leads to the highest performing teams - at every level within the organization.

Real Diversity at Work

• Are you worried about the cultural mix of your employees, or wondering if you have enough difference to make better informed decisions?

• Do you have a diversity agenda, or specific recruitment target to meet?

• Who succeeds in your organization - is it people who look and sound like you?

Your approach to building a diverse workforce focuses on getting diverse teams to work together more cohesively. We consider not only the cultural sensitivity required in a global environment, but also personality, communication styles, and individual strengths. Building a high performing team is like heading out for a round of golf. You don't just take a putter, or a wedge. You take the whole bag of clubs, because the course is likely to be complex and challenging, and your chances of a good game depend on you having a wide toolkit. Each club has been designed for a specific task. A wedge is no good for the tee off, and a putter won't get you out of the rough. If you are working on your handicap, you need to have the widest range of clubs possible. It is the same in business. There are many tools for assessing personality and style in a safe and respectful way. As consultants, we have developed a suite of techniques for understanding individual performance and potential, which is inspiring and perfect for a more tailored management approach. We use a range of psychometric assessments, depending on the needs of client teams. We do strengths profiling too, and run carefully curated activities to test different types in action. We work with clients to build up an impactful personal profile to help build self-awareness, social awareness, more effective workload planning, build individual self-esteem and reduce the risk of conflict derailing your projects.

Case Study - Diversity in an Engineering Team

As part of a major leadership development program with an aerospace client, the sensitive subject of diversity was raised. This client is a fascinating organization, employing very clever people indeed, usually from an engineering background. As part of the leadership program, we used the Myers Briggs Type Indicator psychometric to help pave the way to a discussion about diversity.

Out of 16 participants on the program, 13 returned exactly the same result! As we did 1:1 feedback with each person, it soon became apparent that the team was in fact much more diverse in their personality types, but they had learned how to 'play the game'. "In our business," one person confided in me, "You have to be an ESTJ in order to get on." It was an interesting insight, and the most perfect example of what happens when we fall into the trap of recruiting in our own image. It's human nature, by the way; we want to work with people like us, who think the same way we do. Unfortunately, it has a dangerous tendency to lead to Groupthink, and make life really tough for other team members who don't fit the mould. There was one person in this same team who was the polar opposite of his colleagues, and each time he opened his mouth to make a suggestion, the others glazed over, or rolled their eyes. He stopped participating in the activities, and was always stepping out to take a call, because he felt that nobody was interested in his contribution.

Diversity, as we see it, is about many different human elements. It goes far beyond segmenting an employee base by gender, ethnicity or orientation. Actually, we think it's much more fundamental than that; real diversity is about finding the optimum mix of different personalities, strengths, and experience. If you recruit with that in mind, you will be more likely to recruit a wider mix of ethnicities, a better gender balance, and a wider range of orientations.

We worked with this team to help them understand the brilliant insights offered by the one guy who was different. They learned to appreciate his insights, and he began to appreciate their perspectives. As a result, the team not only worked more cohesively, they became much more aware of their own biases and assumptions about people who were different to them.

Don't preach teamwork and then favour people just because they think the same way as you. It will reward masked behaviour.

Career DNA

Now you have started to understand who you are, let's begin the process of understanding what has brought you to this point.

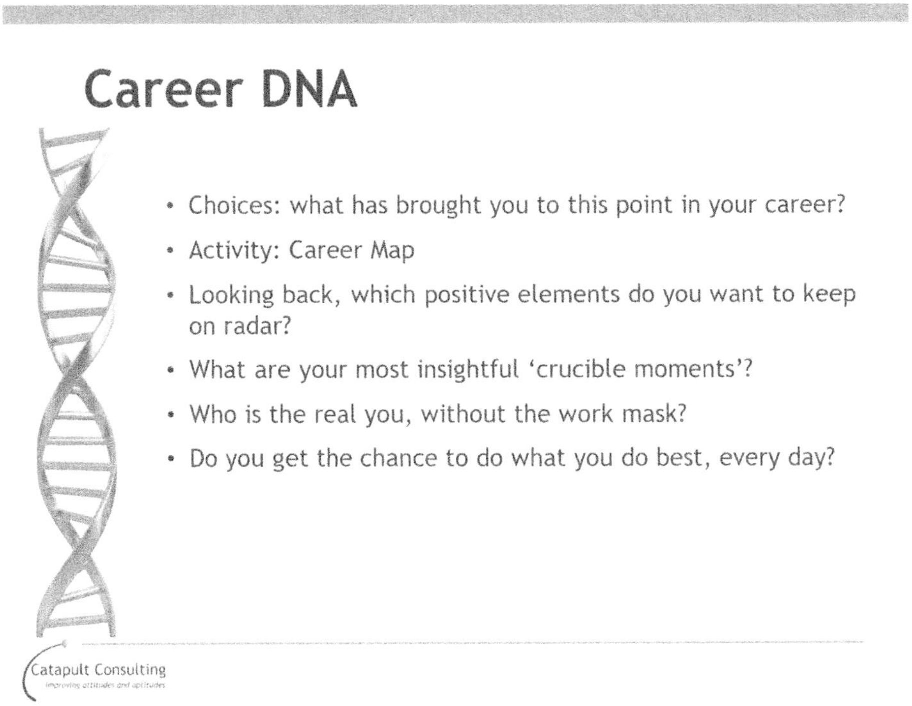

Your Career: A Potted History

Take a moment to write down some of the key points in your professional timeline.

Career Map

This activity provides a profound opportunity to reflect on what has gone before, to understand those things which have had the most negative - and most positive impact on your life, and to learn from it.

Step 1
On the next page you will find a graph, like the one above, where the Y axis (vertical) will measure happiness, from very happy (at the top) to very unhappy (at the bottom), and the X axis (horizontal) measures time, starting from whenever you entered the world of work, to whatever age you are now. Draw a line, charting the highs and lows of your career to date, to coincide with different years of your life. It doesn't need to be too accurate; you are just looking for general trends.

Step 2
Look at each of the high points on your career map. What do each of the highs have in common? Identify at least three things that were present at each high point, for example, happy working relationships, good social life, great boss, work felt meaningful, lived in a nice place. These are things you should have in place in order to thrive.

Step 3
Now examine each of the low points. What three things do they have in common? These are your red flags, things to watch out for. They might include a long commute, or poorly managed work conflict, or financial uncertainty, or health issues. You need to reduce or eliminate these.

Step 4
Go back to the low points, and for each dip, identify at least one way in which you are a stronger person as a result of that difficult time, or made some tough choices which have worked out well. You can't change the past, but changing what you think about it will change how you feel about it, and shape your courage for the future.

My Career Map

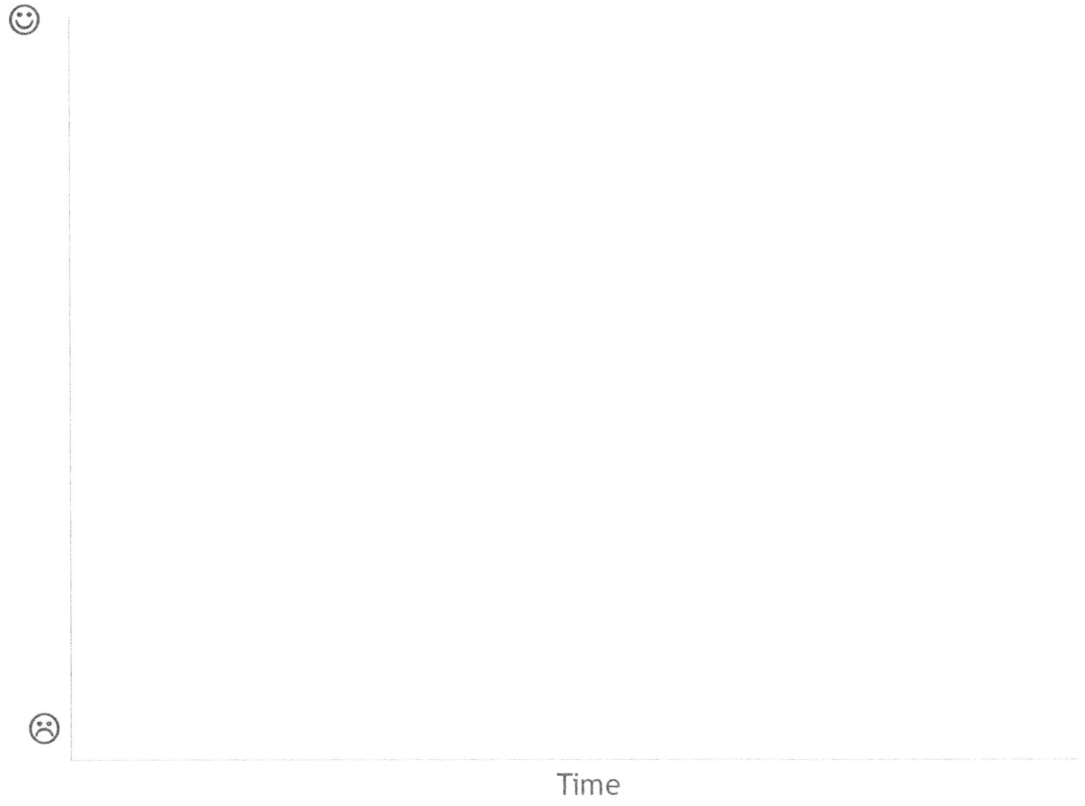

Career high points: what do they have in common?

How can you ensure you make these things a priority, to keep you on top of your game?

How do these 'green flags' tally with your personal values?

Career low points: what do they have in common?

These are your 'red flags'. What steps can you take to address them if they start appearing again?

How might these 'red flags' be in conflict with your personal values?

How have your most difficult 'crucible' moments informed your leadership journey? How has the way you dealt with them made you a better leader?

Strengths-Based Leadership

Now we are going to explore strengths-based leadership as the key to unlocking peak performance.

You might imagine that as a leader, you need to be good at everything. But the jack-of-all-trades is truly the master of none, as the saying goes. The entire philosophy of strengths-based working - developed by Professor Martin Seligman - is that we make greater progress and enjoy our work much more when we get to focus on what we're good at, rather than criticising ourselves for those areas where we don't perform so well.

Strengths

Seligman

- Signature strengths are positive traits that a person owns, celebrates and frequently exercises to achieve a fulfilling life.
- E.g. zest, hope, curiosity, gratitude and love

Gallup's talents and strengths

- Successful managers focus on individual's unique talents and fit the job to it
- Talents can be developed into strengths - "the ability to produce near-perfect performance on a specific task"
- E.g. strategic, activator, winning others over

Catapult Consulting

In order to become familiar with your own personal and professional strengths, you might want to complete a couple of strengths assessments.

1. https://www.authentichappiness.sas.upenn.edu/testcenter will take you to Professor Martin Seligman's own assessment centre, where you can complete a battery of free personality assessments. Seligman's assessment looks at 'Life' strengths. Scroll down to VIA (values in action) Survey of Character Strengths. It's a long questionnaire, so make time to do it properly, all in one go.

What are your top five Life strengths?

-
-
-
-
-

2. Next, you should consider your Work strengths. You will need to purchase a copy of either of the following strengths assessment books, available on Amazon and other places. Please ensure that the copy you buy is **NEW** (not USED).

Each book contains a cut out section with a unique access code. You will need that code to access the test online. It's a great book as well, with lots of information about how to put your strengths to work.

https://www.gallup.com/cliftonstrengths/en/254033/strengthsfinder.aspx

What are your top five Work strengths?

-
-
-
-
-

Is there any duplication between your life strengths and your work strengths? What does that tell you?

Why do you think we look at work strengths on a leadership program?

What happens when you get to use your strengths at work, regularly?

What happens when you get to use your strengths at work only on rare occasions?

Why might leaders take their own strengths for granted?

Historical approach

Historically, professional development has taken a remedial approach

- Correct under-performance
- Fix weaknesses
- Resolve problems
- Plug gaps

- Impact on motivation?
- Fatal flaws v allowable weaknesses

Catapult Consulting

Which weaknesses have you invested time and effort trying to fix?

Putting it to the test

Weakness-based:

- Think of an aspect of your role that you really struggle with, and find a burden.
- Formulate a 12-month plan to bring your performance to an adequate level.

Strengths-based:

- Think of an aspect of your role that you really enjoy and at which you excel
- Formulate a 12-month plan to develop your competence further still.

Catapult Consulting

And what was the outcome for you?

Playing to your own strengths

Strengths you are currently using

- How are you currently using this strength?
- How useful is it in your current organisation?

Scope:

- What scope do you have to use more?
- What specifically can you do to use it more?

Catapult Consulting
improving attitudes and aptitudes

Which of your strengths do you use every day?

How could you be using your strengths more at work, for working towards achieving your career goals?

Helping your team play to their strengths

- Strengths vs. skills within your team?
- Building on strengths is more effective than trying to improve weaknesses
- Psychometrics: insight into link with peak performance?
- VIA signature strengths
- Managing projects: a strengths-based approach
- Appreciative Inquiry is a much more constructive basis for driving performance improvement

Catapult Consulting

Which strengths do your team bring to the organization?

Do they get to use their strengths every day?

How could they be using your strengths more at work, for working towards achieving business goals?

How would that help you, as a leader?

Strengths Resumé

*Personal Summary:*____

Highly energetic, positive and enthusiastic team player. Relates well to other people, and a good leader and motivator. Strong on ideas and new ways of working. Good communicator, presenter, teacher and coach.

*Personal Values:*____

Enthusiasm, affiliation, entrepreneurship, independence, leadership, making a difference, personal and professional growth.

Myers Briggs Type Indicator: __________________________________

ENFP Fun-loving and enthusiastic optimist. Innovative problem-solver who enjoys developing visions of the future through sharing thoughts and ideas with others. In tune with others' emotional needs and use this insight to create possibilities for growth and development. Valuing relationships, works best in a flexible and harmonious environment full of opportunity.

*Strengths:*____

Creativity, ingenuity and originality

A mind that is always looking for connections, good at finding new perspectives on familiar challenges. Derives energy when a new idea occurs. May be labelled by others as creative, original or conceptual.

Curiosity and interest in the world

Curious about everything, finds all subjects and topics fascinating. Enjoys exploration and discovery and loves being anywhere there is an opportunity to learn.

Hope, optimism and future-mindedness

Fascinated by strengths - own and others. Look to nurture, refine and stretch others, seeking to capitalize on natural talent and abilities. Always expect the best in the future and work to achieve it. I believe that the future is something that is within my control.

Strategic thinker

Ability to sort through the clutter and find the best route; mindful of patterns and playing out different scenarios, then making selections. What if - select - strike.

Winning people over, networker

Enjoy meeting and initiating with strangers. Rarely at a loss for words, like to find common areas of interest, and build rapport. Find meeting new people very energising.

Create Your Own Strengths Resumé

Personal Summary: ____

Personal Values: ____

Myers Briggs Type Indicator: ______________________________________

*Strengths:*____

How will you use your strengths CV?

Who will you send it to?

How could you use a strengths CV with your team?

How could you use your strengths CV to become a better leader?

Now print off your strengths CV, and compare it with your job description. If you were recruiting for your role, would you recruit you? Are you in the right role?

Many of our clients report that they use their strengths CV when applying for a new job. Several have commented that focusing the interview on their strengths creates such a positive impression on the interviewers that it sometimes results in being promoted two levels up! We now teach this at Warwick University and on all leadership programs.

Understanding 'derailers'

Something that gets in the way of our progress; more than just a weakness

Potential to limit progress

Catapult Consulting

How can you mitigate for some of your lesser weaknesses?

Which of your derailers do you need to address, as a matter of priority?

Leading Different Generations

We have looked at how heterogeneous teams outperform homogeneous teams, and considered our differences through the lenses of personality and strengths. But what about different generations? It is highly likely that you will have leadership responsibility for a range of different people from different generations, and it is dangerously easy to make snap judgements about them.

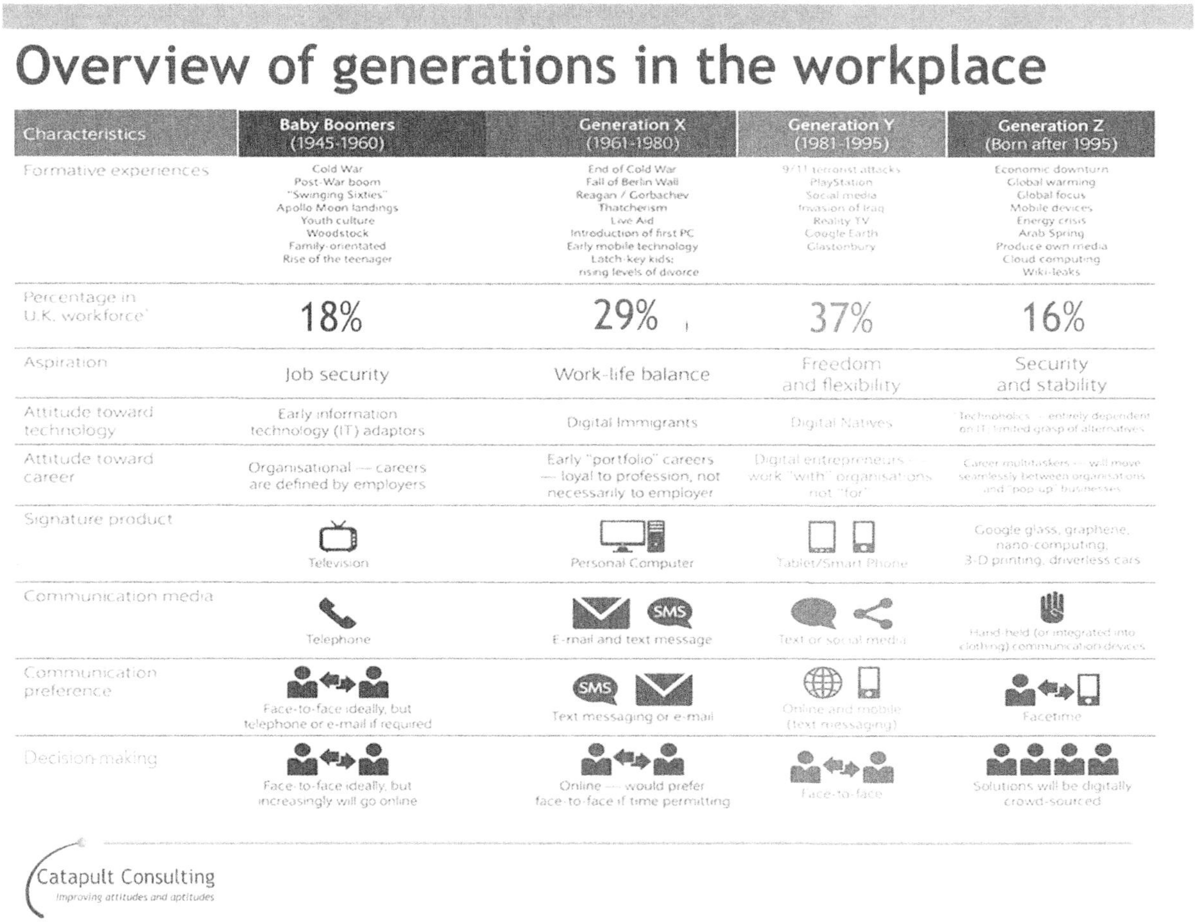

Overview of generations in the workplace

Characteristics	Baby Boomers (1945-1960)	Generation X (1961-1980)	Generation Y (1981-1995)	Generation Z (Born after 1995)
Formative experiences	Cold War Post-War boom "Swinging Sixties" Apollo Moon landings Youth culture Woodstock Family-orientated Rise of the teenager	End of Cold War Fall of Berlin Wall Reagan / Gorbachev Thatcherism Live Aid Introduction of first PC Early mobile technology Latch-key kids; rising levels of divorce	9/11 terrorist attacks PlayStation Social media Invasion of Iraq Reality TV Google Earth Glastonbury	Economic downturn Global warming Global focus Mobile devices Energy crisis Arab Spring Produce own media Cloud computing Wiki-leaks
Percentage in U.K. workforce'	18%	29%	37%	16%
Aspiration	Job security	Work-life balance	Freedom and flexibility	Security and stability
Attitude toward technology	Early information technology (IT) adaptors	Digital Immigrants	Digital Natives	Technoholics — entirely dependent on IT; limited grasp of alternatives
Attitude toward career	Organisational — careers are defined by employers	Early "portfolio" careers — loyal to profession, not necessarily to employer	Digital entrepreneurs — work "with" organisations not "for"	Career multitaskers — will move seamlessly between organisations and "pop-up" businesses
Signature product	Television	Personal Computer	Tablet/Smart Phone	Google glass, graphene, nano-computing, 3-D printing, driverless cars
Communication media	Telephone	E-mail and text message	Text or social media	Hand-held (or integrated into clothing) communication devices
Communication preference	Face-to-face ideally, but telephone or e-mail if required	Text messaging or e-mail	Online and mobile (text messaging)	Facetime
Decision-making	Face-to-face ideally, but increasingly will go online	Online — would prefer face-to-face if time permitting	Face-to-face	Solutions will be digitally crowd-sourced

Catapult Consulting
Improving attitudes and aptitudes

This graphic provides some helpful context for each generation and offers some useful insight into how we may need to lead them differently.

What considerations will you need to make in order to lead different generations effectively?

Leadership or Management?

1. Take each of the activities in the envelope, and sort them into 3 piles:
   - I do this every day
   - I do this sometimes
   - I never do this
2. Take the following roles and responsibilities and place them on the graph
   - Which elements take up most of your time?
   - Are you truly a leader, or do you spend most of your time stuck in the operational management details?

Catapult Consulting
Improving attitudes and aptitudes

Over the page, you will see various activities listed. Please cut out the page and then cut along the lines as indicated to separate out each activity, before arranging as instructed.

Reviewing individual performance	Identifying strategy	Helping people to succeed	Allocating tasks to people	Setting expectations for behavior
Securing resources	Maintaining professional relationships	Keeping staff informed	Challenging accepted practices	Acting as a role model
Focusing on customers	Prioritizing tasks	Empowering others to do their jobs	Identifying solutions	Motivating people
Establishing a network of contacts	Delivering difficult messages	Shaping culture	Resolving disputes	Harnessing the talents of others
Managing budgets	Describing an inspiring mission	Analysing problems	Developing people	Looking ahead
Taking a stand when needed	Planning and scheduling	Communicating a vision for change	Addressing poor performance	Reporting on progress
Explaining the business context	Being true to your personal values	Ensuring strategic alignment	Influencing behavior	Building best practice

Leadership or Management?

What do you notice about the distribution of your activities?

How are you spending most of your time at work?

How will you shift your focus to move into leadership?

Leadership or Management?

Leadership: relationship (not ownership)

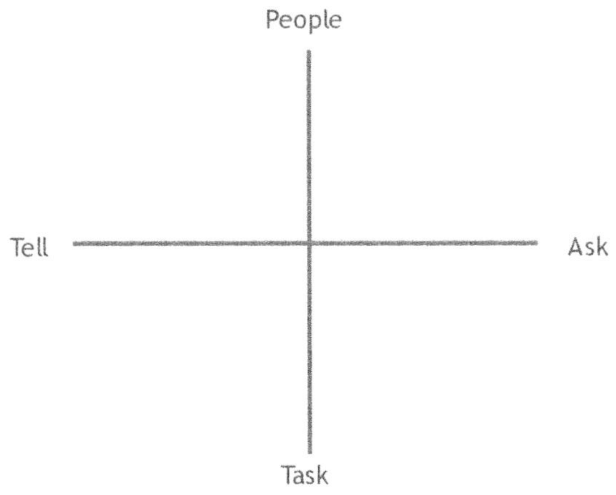

Catapult Consulting

In which quadrant do you spend most of your time?

What do you want to remember about this activity?

What are the consequences of failing to make time to lead?

Nobody will give you time to lead, you have to prioritize it for yourself. How do you plan to do that?

Workload Prioritization

In order to make time for leadership, you need to know how you are currently spending your time at work.

Workload Audit

- Take 10 minutes to note down a list of all the activities you have to do at work
- Then transfer that list onto the four box model

Catapult Consulting

The Eisenhower prioritization matrix was used by Eisenhower to help him manage the weighty responsibility of presidency. He knew there was more for him to do than he ever had time to accommodate, so he prioritized to ensure he was working on the most important tasks.

Workload Prioritisation

Catapult Consulting

This is how managers in a typical organization prioritize their responsibilities.

And THIS is how effective leaders manage their time. The biggest shift is from "urgent, but not important" towards "important, but not urgent".

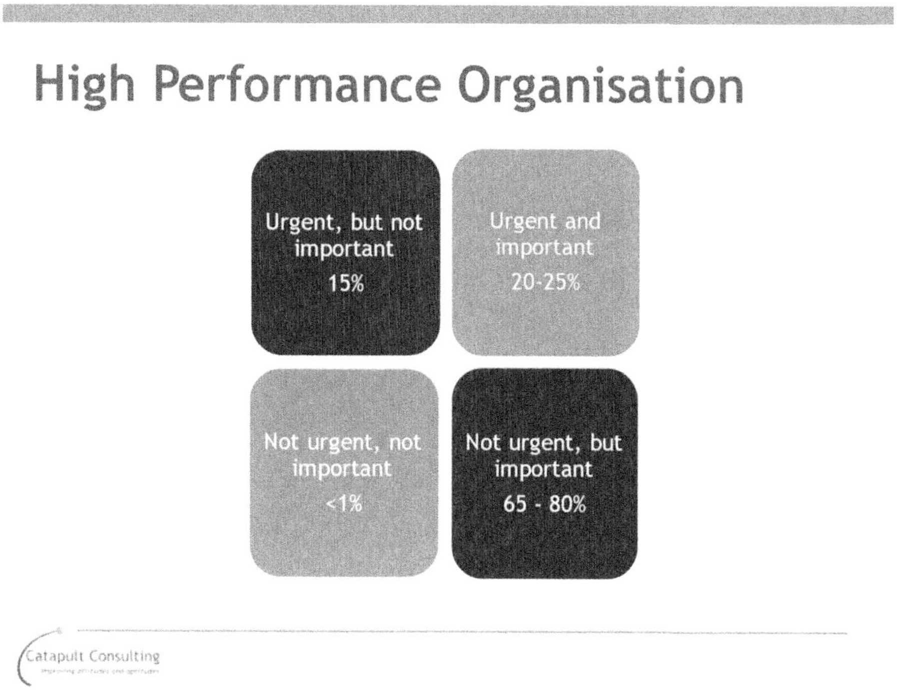

Prioritising workload

Unless you prioritise effectively, you will never make time for leadership.

Catapult Consulting

Populate this matrix with all the tasks on your current to-do list:

URGENT, BUT NOT IMPORTANT	URGENT & IMPORTANT
NEITHER URGENT NOR IMPORTANT	NOT URGENT, BUT IMPORTANT

What a big difference we can make with effective prioritization!

- Take a moment to think about all the tasks you are required to complete over the course of a month. Which task belongs in which box, now?

#1: URGENT & IMPORTANT

#2: NOT URGENT, BUT IMPORTANT

#3: URGENT BUT NOT IMPORTANT

#4: NOT URGENT, NOT IMPORTANT

Write it down.

It is not enough simply to THINK about the tasks in priority order - you must write them down, otherwise you may forget important items. You can write it on a piece of paper, on a flip chart or a white board next to your desk. Wherever you write it, put it somewhere very visible so that you can check your list on a daily basis, and prioritize each morning, depending on the needs of the business. Also, it will serve as a good example to your teams.

Tip:

When someone comes to you and asks you to complete an urgent task for them, you can show them your prioritization matrix, and tell them where it fits with your current task list, and the time you have available. If the list is only in your head, it may appear that you are making excuses and being uncooperative.

If you also add the initials of the person for whom you are doing each task onto your list, it can help to stop people queue-jumping. If somebody comes rushing into your office demanding you do an urgent task for them, you can refer them to your prioritization matrix. Not only can they see that you already have a full workload for the day, but they can also see who you are working for. If they are more senior than the other names on your list, they probably have the right to ask you to do their task first. If they are less senior than the names on your list, they will be more likely to go and ask someone else, instead.

- How can you use this to make sure you are putting the most important work at the very top of your to-do list?

- And how can you use this to help your people focus on the most important things... every... single... day?

Leading on Purpose

- Leadership is earned, it is not for the faint -hearted
- It is a vocation like any other, and should be freely chosen, and not imposed
- You cannot lead authentically unless you know who you are, what you stand for, and where you want to go
- The aims of this module - to hold up the mirror
- Common vision, common purpose
- Inspirational leadership fit for the 21 st Century

Catapult Consulting

Future Career Trajectory

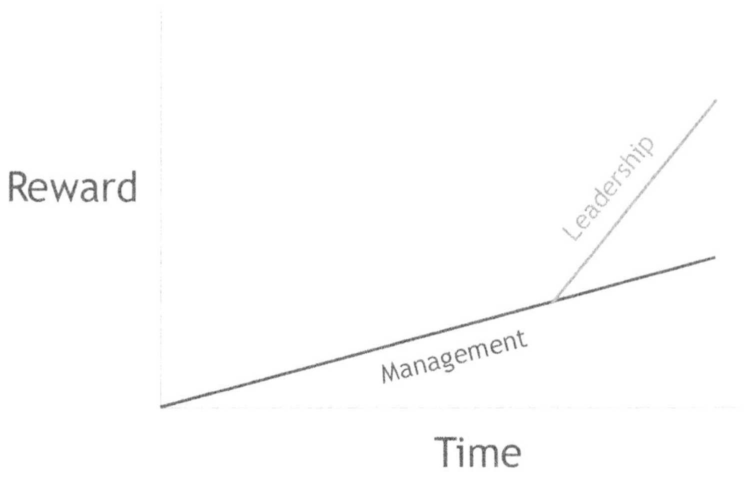

Catapult Consulting

Authentic Leadership: finding your True North

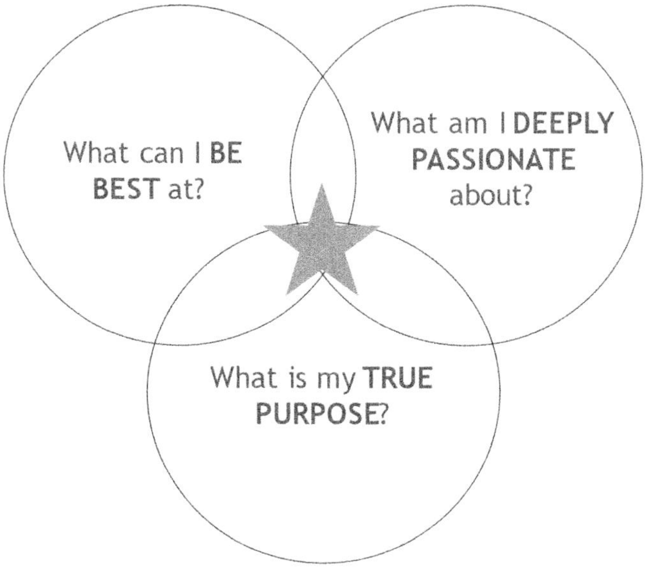

Catapult Consulting

How would you populate this model for yourself? Take a moment and draw out these three circles onto a larger piece of paper, and think about what belongs in each circle, for a truly personal insight into finding your true north.

True North

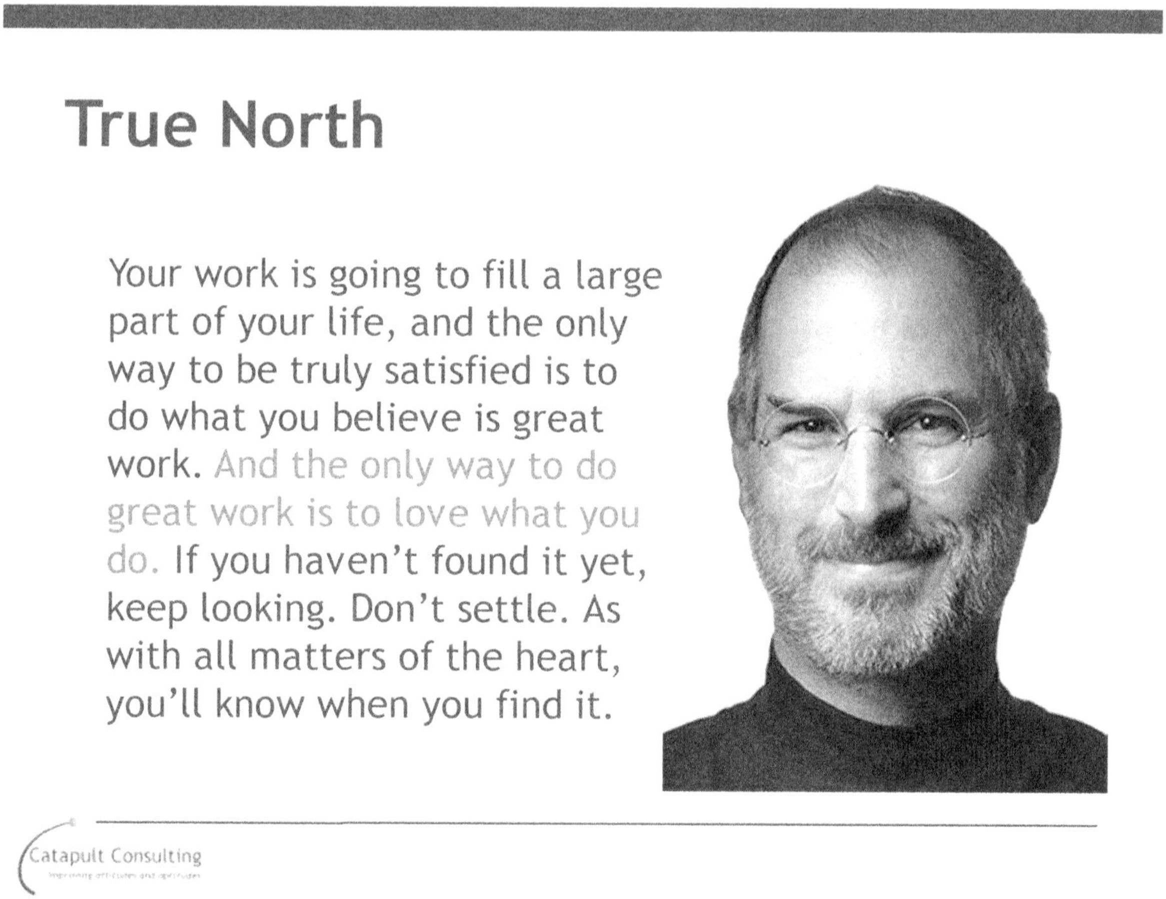

Is it possible for you to do work you love?

What might get in the way of doing work you love?

What do you want to remember about the above slide?

What have been your biggest insights from part one?

What do you want to think about further?
(Create a to-think list, not just a to-do list!)

What actions will you take to put your ideas into practice?

When will you take those actions?

Who will hold you accountable?

What obstacles can you anticipate which might prevent you from achieving your action plan?

What steps can you take to ensure that those obstacles don't prevent you from making the significant progress expected of you?

Personal Reflection

Think about what you have learned about yourself, your style and impact, and the habits you have developed, and how you will integrate this learning to raise your leadership game.

Part Two: Leading Others

How much can you recall from part one?

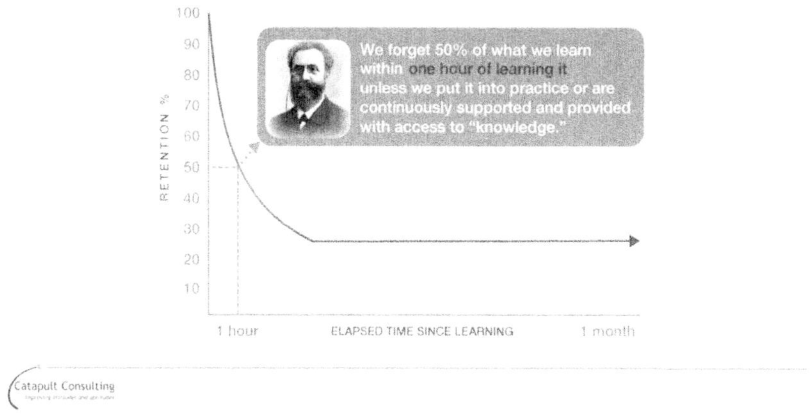

How much of the learning from part one can you still remember?

Take a few minutes to read back through your workbook, and pick out your key learning points so far.

In part two, we are going to explore putting the learning from part one into the context of your team and your leadership practice.

Part Two: Leading Others

- Recap on Module One
- Leadership models
- Conflict management
- Motivation - the psychological contract
- Building a high performance team
- Managing different generations
- Crucible conversations: the key to managing performance
- Communicating like a Boss
- Coaching for peak performance
- Leadership Manifesto

Catapult Consulting

VUCA World

Leaders: This is YOUR BIG MOMENT!

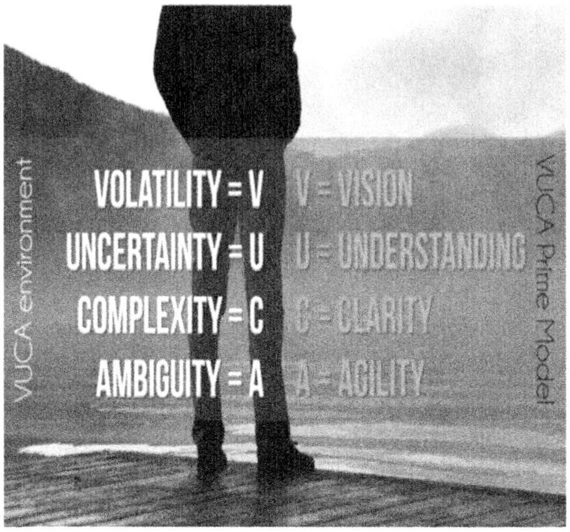

Catapult Consulting

In the 1980s, the U.S. military coined the term VUCA to describe the climate in which they were operating. They observed that the world was a volatile, uncertain, complex and ambiguous place, and that military strategy needed to reflect that.

40 years later, the world has become even more volatile, uncertain, complex and ambiguous, and this state applies particularly within our organizations as well. The only sensible response to this external situation, then, is to lead by articulating a compelling vision for the future, to show understanding about how unsettling continuous change can be, to provide clarity on the link between the day job and achieving the vision, clarity of expectations and clarity in feedback on performance, and finally to create an organizational culture of agility to respond to the changing nature of the external business context.

In a VUCA world, how will you lead with vision, understanding, clarity and agility?

How we Create Corporate Culture

- 5 gorillas in a cage
- Everything we say and everything we do
- How would you sum up your culture?
    - Cultural norms, traditions, assumptions, dynamics
- Psychological safety - permission to make mistakes
- Gap analysis: where are we now? Where do we need to get to?
- 'Sacred Cows' make the best burgers!
- Hofstede on international culture

Catapult Consulting

Five Gorillas in a Cage

One way to explain organizational culture is through the story of a piece of research into social integration.

Researchers placed five gorillas together in a cage in order to study their behavior. These gorillas were well fed, healthy and socialized. In the ceiling of the cage was a hook holding a bunch of bananas, and we all know that gorillas love bananas! However, each time one of the gorillas reached up for a banana, the researchers sprayed all of the gorillas with cold water. They sprayed until the gorilla left the bananas alone. The gorillas quickly learnt to manage the bananas, stopping any gorilla who fancied a snack, in order to avoid all being sprayed with cold water.

Eventually, one of the gorillas was removed from the cage and replaced with a new (also socialised) gorilla. The new gorilla saw the bananas and reached up, but the other gorillas got angry and prevented him from reaching them. He had no idea of why he was attacked, but quickly learnt not to touch the bananas. Eventually, all of the original gorillas were replaced with new gorillas, none of whom had experienced the cold-water treatment, but who all knew that touching the bananas was forbidden.

That is how organizational culture develops. We have company rules, rituals and routines which might once have served the business well, but the business context has changed, and yet the longer serving staff may still try to reinforce outmoded habits. The role of the leader is to identify these 'sacred cow' habits, and gently challenge them. That is how organizational culture evolves.

How would you describe the culture at your organization?

What are the Sacred Cows (unspoken rules) at your organization?

How well are they serving the business?

The Cultural Iceberg:

What we can see, we can deal with. It's what's below the waterline that can sink us.

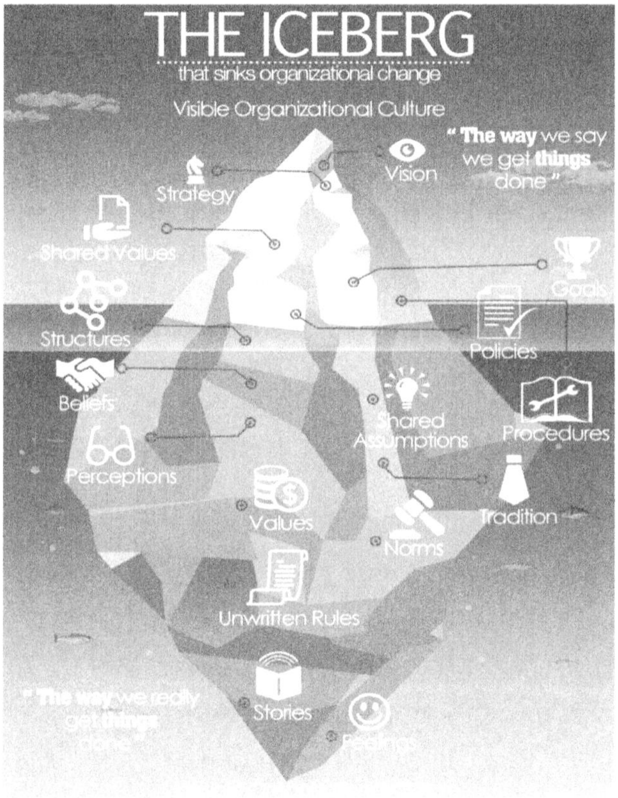

What are the biggest cultural challenges in your organization?

What do you want to do about it?

Leaders shape culture. So where does leadership come from?

Leaders: Nature or Nurture?

Nature:	Nurture:
Leadership as a birth right Natural-born leaders are attractive and commanding They naturally gravitate towards leadership, and others naturally follow	Leadership is a choice Leaders possess vision Leadership is situational Status is earned Built on trust and credibility Leadership skills are learned and developed

Catapult Consulting

Which sort of leaders succeed at your organization? Natural-born leaders, or those who have grown and developed into leadership?

Eight Primary Leadership Styles

From most to least successful in the long run

- Democratic
- Affiliative
- Coaching
- Pacesetting
- Authoritative
- Charismatic
- Autocratic
- Laissez-faire

Catapult Consulting

Which of these leadership styles is most commonly observed within your business?

Which one will be your go-to style?

Democratic Leadership

- **The pros:**
- Creativity and innovation are encouraged
- Collaboration creates strong multi -disciplinary solutions for complex issues
- High employee engagement and involvement.
- Higher productivity and accountability.
- **The cons:**
- Can cause confusion, delays and conflict.
- Can lack focus and direction.
- Some ideas may get more attention than others, causing resentment.
- Collaborative decision -making is time-consuming.
- The team may have limited expertise or experience.
- Employees can get too used to being involved in decision -making and expect to be included in all decisions.

Catapult Consulting

Which leaders can you think of who use this style of leadership?

Under which conditions might it be the best approach?

Affiliative Leadership

- The pros:
- Offers more opportunities for diversity.
- Builds trust within an organisation.
- Strengthens cross-functional working relationships.
- Recognises and rewards people skills.
- Teams handle emotional challenges better.
- Employees experience less stress and higher autonomy.
- The cons:
- Potential power struggles between departmental leaders.
- Can hamper results, prioritising people over the task in hand.
- Underperformance can be overlooked, resulting in low standards.
- Can foster a sense of favouritism and frustration.
- Lacks clear direction in times of crisis.

Catapult Consulting

Which leaders can you think of who use this style of leadership?

Under which conditions might it be the best approach?

Coaching Leadership

The pros:
•Encourages two-way communication and collaboration.
•Helps people improve their skills so that they can perform at their best.
•Objectives and goals are clear.
•Having support is motivating to individuals and groups
•Helps to identify weaknesses, and transform them into strengths.
•Enables organisations to develop talent and grow a highly skilled workforce.
•Promotes trust and empowerment.

The cons:
•Requires a lot of one-to-one time and patience.
•Doesn't always lead to the fastest, most efficient results.
•The leader needs confidence and skill to give meaningful feedback
•Leaders often have to prioritise achieving their own goals, and coaching takes a lower priority which can be demotivating for the team.
•Team members are not committed to the process.

Catapult Consulting

Which leaders can you think of who use this style of leadership?

Under which conditions might it be the best approach?

Pacesetting Leadership

The pros:

- Highly self-motivated and a strong desire to succeed.
- Reaching time critical, short-term results.
- Leading teams that need little direction or co-ordination.
- Inspiring high performance, high pace and high quality.

The cons:

- Values results more than anything, including the team.
- Detrimental for employee engagement and motivation in the long run.
- Individuals can feel stressed, overwhelmed and receive little or no feedback or development.

Catapult Consulting

Which leaders can you think of who use this style of leadership?

Under which conditions might it be the best approach?

Authoritative Leadership

The pros :
Motivating for the team.
Beneficial for building strong relationships and encouraging collaboration.
Empowers team members with autonomy to do their jobs.
Can lead to more creativity and innovation.

The cons:
Pressure on the leader, who needs to lead by example.
Can cause feelings of instability by disrupting the status quo
May not be a good culture fit for a more "traditional hierarchical" organisational culture.

Catapult Consulting

Which leaders can you think of who use this style of leadership?

Under which conditions might it be the best approach?

Autocratic Leadership

The pros

•Can be efficient, especially when it comes to decision -making.

•One person taking charge can keep teams cohesive and consistent.

•Can reduce individual stress by the leader making decisions quickly.

•Makes roles clearer since they are delegated specific duties

The cons

Can stifle creativity, collaboration, innovation.

•Highly stressful because the leader is responsible for everything.

•Inflexibility leads to resentment by followers

•Can lead to Groupthink

Catapult Consulting

Which leaders can you think of who use this style of leadership?

Under which conditions might it be the best approach?

Charismatic Leadership

The pros

- Engages the heart by connecting with things people really care about
- Highly relatable
- Creates viral advocacy

The cons

Need to check motives!

May be impractical

Can be insincere and manipulative

Can lead good people to do bad things

Catapult Consulting

Which leaders can you think of who use this style of leadership?

Under which conditions might it be the best approach?

Laissez-faire Leadership

- **The pros :**
- Encourages trust between team members and leader.
- Inspires independent thinking and acting.
- Less fear of failure.
- Can lead to increased creativity and innovation.
- Empowers individuals.
- **The cons :**
- Leaders can appear too distant and unapproachable.
- Can result in low productivity.
- Not effective with unskilled or unmotivated individuals.
- Conflict can occur between team members.
- Team members may vie to fill the leadership void.

Catapult Consulting

Which leaders can you think of who use this style of leadership?

Under which conditions might it be the best approach?

Contextual Leadership

Leaders who have been extremely successful in one organization, sometimes find themselves headhunted into another, where they do not thrive at all.

What are the possible reasons for this?

Business Lifecycle

The leadership style best suited to the start-up and high growth phase is different from the style of leadership required to manage an organization through plateau and stagnation, which is different again from the style of leadership to help rescue an organization from decline, and reinvigorate it.

Match your leadership style to the business phase, and see where you can have most impact.

Organizations often make the mistake of leaving it too late to hire a different leader.

Unless the organization is brutally honest with itself, it is likely to hire a star leader from another organization but not necessarily in the part of the business lifecycle to which their new star is best suited.

And remember, the failure of your business is a failure of leadership.

Leaders are personally accountable

Catapult Consulting

If you are not accountable, and instead, make excuses for your errors - your credibility will get quickly called into question! Own your mistakes; people will respect you more for it.

If your organization is not performing at its best, are you owning the part you have to play in that situation?

How can you increase your personal accountability for the performance of the business and the outcomes you achieve?

How can you encourage greater accountability across your leadership and management teams?

Ownership & Accountability

High performance culture can only be achieved where employees have a strong sense of personal accountability. A blame culture, excuses, avoidance and back-stabbing are symptoms of a highly toxic culture.

The most successful people are those with really high levels of personal accountability, who do not blame others for their choices.

Mindset is a matter of choice. We can choose to feel like the victim in a challenging situation, or we can take ownership for the part we played in the situation.

When people are stuck in the Victim mindset, they say things like...

- It wasn't my fault.
- The guy never got back to me
- I was too busy
- Someone else let me down
- That wasn't my job
- I don't remember agreeing to that

When people have high personal accountability, they say things like...

- I said I would do it, so even though it wasn't my responsibility, I did it.
- The guy didn't get back to me, so I went and found out who else could help
- I was very busy, but I prioritised it because I knew it was important
- That person let me down, so I spoke to someone else and resolved it that way
- It took some digging, but finally I found it.
- It's entirely my fault. I completely forgot. I'm very sorry.

What is the language you are hearing from the employees in your team?

How will you challenge victim mindset?

Promoting Ownership & Accountability

- Role model the change you want from others
- Incentivise and reward the right behaviours
- Consequences game: in their words
- Pre-mortem
- Who, why, what, when, where, how?
- "Towards" / "Away from" language
- Micro Leadership
- Stand ups
- Check commitment
- SMART objectives
- Signpost why some people leave (if appropriate)
- Million dollar question

Catapult Consulting

Help the person to think through the consequences of a particular course of action before they begin. That way, you can anticipate what might go wrong, and decide on a different path.

A pre-mortem helps you to anticipate what could go wrong with a plan, and to put steps in place to overcome those obstacles.

Using 'towards' language - saying what you want them to do - is much more effective than 'away from' language - telling them what you don't want them to do.

The million-dollar question works well for people who keep saying that they can't do something. Ask them if they could do it for $1M and they will usually be able to find a way!

We will discuss micro-leadership later on. (Spoiler alert: it's not just better-paid micro-management!)

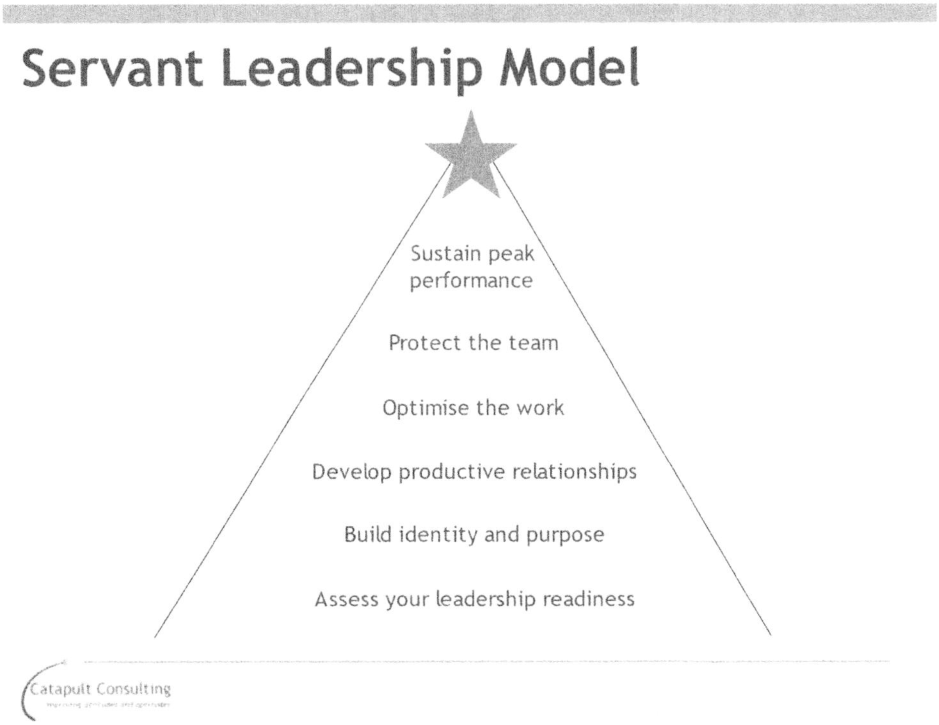

Robert Greenleaf (1977) proposed the idea that the best way to lead was to give the team what they need in order to perform, and then to get out of their way. Despite myriad new theories in leadership, it is Servant Leadership which works best, especially during periods of change and uncertainty.

How would that work for you?

What would get in the way of servant leadership in your organization?

Servant Leadership

Is...

- Having pure motives
- "What's in it for US?"
- Helping and empowering others
- Humility and character
- Highest levels of integrity
- Accountability for own mistakes

Is not...

- Extrinsic motivation
- "What's in it for ME?"
- Personal credit and status
- Complacent about abilities
- Justifies poor decisions
- Shifts blame
- "That's just the way I am; I can't change!"

Catapult Consulting

Is your organization ready for servant leadership?

Are you ready for leadership?

1. Assess your Leadership Readiness

- First: select your career trajectory
- Honest self-evaluation: identity and purpose
- Examine your strengths, priorities, aspirations, competences and experiences
- Be honest about your motives
- Explore your values, attitudes and beliefs
- Invite, receive and digest formal feedback
- Work with a personal board of directors
- Assess your support network and sphere of influence
- Understand your career derailers
- Honest appraisal of your emotional intelligence

Catapult Consulting

Following part one, do you feel that you are ready for a leadership role?

What do you need to work on to ensure that you are 'match-fit'?

How will you use your strengths to guide your leadership?

TOOLKIT

2. Build Identity and Purpose

- Know the vision
- Inspire a shared vision
- Clarify vision and goals with others
- Collaborate on project objectives
- Foster a team ethos

Catapult Consulting

Are you clear on the difference between your business vision (for the future) and mission (why you exist)?

Could you explain your vision and goals to others, right now?

If not, what do you need to know in order to develop a clearer understanding, ready to share with your employees?

Catapult Consulting

You CAN'T lead if you don't know the vision, mission and strategy.

Strategic Framework

1. OVERALL PURPOSE OF THE ORGANISATION	2. BUSINESS CONTEXT	3. COMPETITIVE BUSINESS STRATEGY	4. DIRECTORATE/ DEPT PLAN	5. RESOURCING STRATEGY
What is our vision, our mission and our core values? • The value proposition; what are we offering? • What are the overriding goals of this organisation?	(external forces driving change) • PESTLE analysis • TOWS external analysis Threats and opportunities Analysis of current internal capability to deliver • TOWS internal analysis of current capability to respond to external forces Weaknesses Strengths	State 1 or 2 realistic strategies, e.g. Merger and acquisition, Research & development, Increasing production, entering into a new market, increasing market share Identify 3 - 5 strategic imperatives	Summary statement of how this dept / directorate works to deliver business goals Identify 5 - 8 strategic goals which clearly align to business goals Break down into more manageable sub goals for specific teams	Resourcing issues: current and anticipated Can the people resource deliver the business goals? Identify the challenges that need to be addressed. e.g. R&D- 1. Buy in expertise. 2. Raise skills through training 3. Strong performance management 4. Increase employee engagement 3. Build a conducive organisational culture that allows employees to work creatively motivation, managing work life balance.

Catapult Consulting
Improving attitudes and aptitudes

Box 1: Overall purpose of the Organization: "The perfect world is one where...."

Our Mission: "We can make that vision a reality by ...."

Our Strategy: "We will achieve this by...."

CHECK! Does each member of the executive leadership team have the same understanding / agreement with these fundamental elements? If not, your efforts will become diluted.

Our Organization

Our Vision:

Our Mission:

Our Values:

Our Strategic Imperatives:

Need help completing any of these? Ask your line manager, or a member of the Executive Team. Still no straight answer? Draft your thoughts about what it could be, and check with your line manager.

Next, let's look at the business context

When deciding on the strategic direction of the organization, you must first consider the external and internal influences on the likely success of your business. The macro environment is very difficult to influence, but crucial to understand when devising your strategy.

Box 2. Business Context

One model for a thorough evaluation of the competitive landscape is the PESTLE analysis. Below are some of the questions you should consider in order to be certain you have done a thorough analysis. The list is not exhaustive, and it is likely that there will be specific questions relating to your products and services and target market which are not covered here.

Political:

- What political factors would we need to consider?
- How could the current global situation make trading easier or tougher?
- What political sensitivities might we need to take into consideration throughout our supply chain?
- How stable are the governments in our target markets?
- What political tensions exist between our country and theirs?

Environmental:

- How is climate change affecting our consumers right now?
- What is the environmental impact of our products and services?
- How are our competitors being drawn into the spotlight for their green credentials?
- What is our target market's approach to recycling: how will they view our organization?
- How sensitive are they to our environmental record?

Social:

- What social trends could impact on our success?
- What consumer attitudes exist within our desired marketplace?
- What do we know about the habits of our target market?
- Who and what do they care about, that we should care about, too?
- Who are their role models and influences?

Technological:

- How might technological developments help or hinder our plans for growth?
- What relevant technological innovations are our customers already using?
- Do they desire a higher level of automation than we can provide?
- What is their approach to flexible (remote) working?
- Are we able to source all the components we need to make our products?

Legal:

- What changes are there (current or planned) to the law which might impact upon our ability to trade?
- What trading policies have they previously enforced or relaxed?
- Will trading with our target market put us in conflict with any of our other trading partners through restrictive trading clauses, for example?
- Is there any anti-trust legislation which we will need to understand?
- What regulatory bodies/organizations exist which we will need to understand?

Economic:

- How healthy is our national economy at the moment?
- What about our target markets - how economically healthy are they?
- Will our customers choose to afford our products and services in the current climate?
- Are there any specific trade or taxation policies which might impact our business profitability?
- What are the current rates of unemployment, inflation and foreign currency exchange in our target markets?

SWOT Analysis

You've probably heard of the SWOT analysis. It stands for Strengths, Weaknesses, Opportunities and Threats.

But it should probably be a TOWS analysis instead! Start by understanding the external threats and opportunities, and only then can you reflect on your company's strengths and weaknesses and decide if you are fit enough to succeed!

Threats (external)	Opportunities (external)
Weaknesses (internal)	**Strengths (internal)**

Box 3: Competitive Business Strategy

Now it's time to decide on the most appropriate business strategy in response to the external pressures that you can't change, and the internal factors which you can.

Possible business strategies:

- Growth through merger and acquisition
- Sell existing products and services to new customers to increase market share
- Sell different products to your existing customers
- Invest heavily in the research and development to create innovative products which are hard to imitate, thereby making the competition irrelevant
- Increase production to benefit from economies of scale, meaning that you can compete on price
- Build the service offering of your company, to meet more of your customer needs than your competitors can
- Design your product to be the very best quality available on the market, to sell to customers who are not price-sensitive
- Outsource your products so that you can supply them quicker than the competition whilst remaining flexible to the changing tastes of your consumers

This generic list covers several different strategic approaches, but the best strategy for your organization may be a combination of two or more, or indeed something completely different.

When you have decided on your strategic approach, you will need to set some goals, for example on cost, profit margins, time to market, desired market share.

Once again, you need to check with your executive team that they are all agreed on the choice of business strategy. Lack of alignment will lead to lack of focus.

Box 4: Directorate / Department Strategic Plan

With a sound understanding of the commercial landscape and a clearly defined business strategy, you are now ready to take the strategy into each directorate. Every director will need to decide upon a set of strategic imperatives for their part of the business to ensure that what they do and how they do it will achieve the business goals.

Our business strategy:

My department strategic plan (which will deliver the business strategy):

Box 5: Resourcing

Now that you have a clear understanding of the external business context, the strategic direction of the company, and have worked up a strategic plan for your part of the business, you need to make sure you have sufficient resources to deliver the plan.

When considering your resourcing, you may wish to think about the following sources of human capital:

1. Do you currently have enough people to deliver your strategic plan?
2. Do you have issues of under-performance within your teams? If so, this is your top priority to address. If all of your people are working effectively, you may find that you have enough resource already.
3. Are there high potential employees working in other departments who are ready for a new challenge? Be sure to discuss such a transfer with that employee's line manager before you go poaching their staff!
4. Do you need to hire in highly skilled experts to deliver your strategic plan? If so, will they be full-time, part-time, fixed-term contractors, 100% outsourced, working in the office, or remotely?
5. If you wish to hire experts, do you have sufficient budget to pay the higher salaries?
6. Would it be cheaper to hire less skilled workers and then train them up to the right level?
7. What is the lead time to recruit the staff you need? Can you get them on board quickly enough to get started?
8. Do any of your existing employees know of friends or associates who might like to join your team? This will save you the agency finder-fee, and often results in the recruitment of people who fit easily into the business culture.
9. It is good practice to discuss your resourcing plans with your colleagues, as they may be able to make helpful suggestions and recommendations for how to cover the workload.

Remember, stress and burnout are at an all-time high, costing organizations millions of dollars of lost working days every year. Don't overload your people, or motivation and performance will drop rapidly.

Lateral AND Linear Alignment

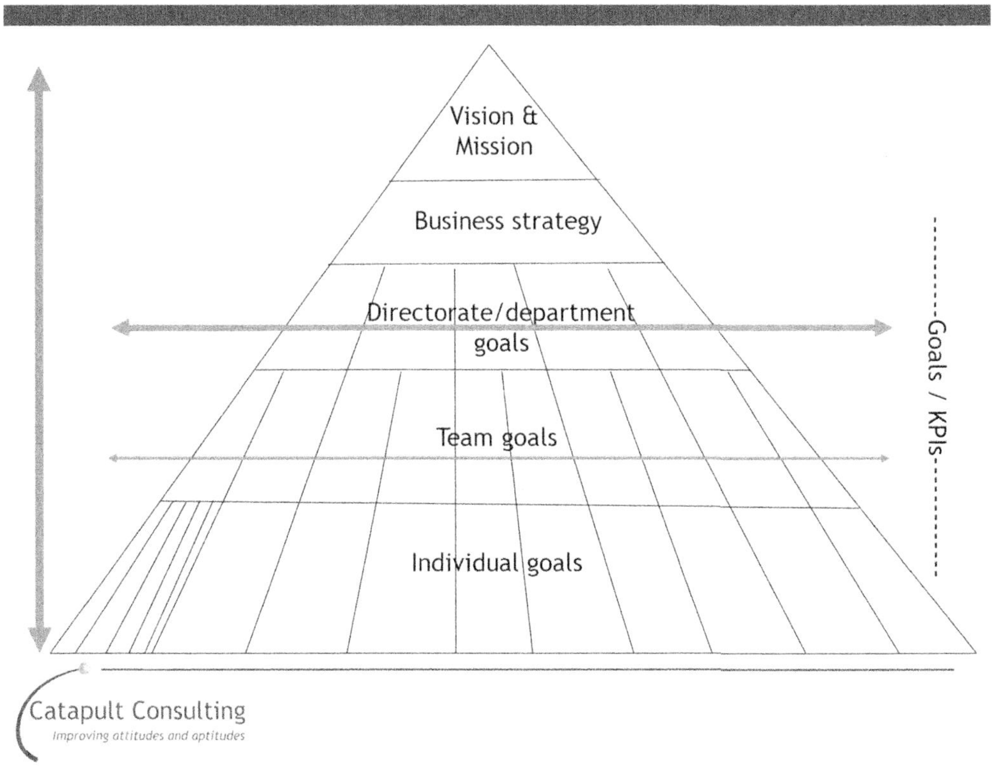

Finally, check on alignment with colleagues

One incredibly useful element of strategic planning is to get all the directors in a room to discuss their own strategic and resourcing plans. This helps to ensure alignment with the common business strategy, and also serves to ensure that one director achieving his goals doesn't inadvertently prevent another director from achieving hers.

This process also helps to ensure that each director understands the contribution made by their colleagues, and will work more collaboratively across the business, reducing silo mentality and ensuring that cross-functional projects and teams are appropriately resourced.

Once this activity has happened at director level, then it should also take place with operational managers, for all of the same reasons.

Now you have created your department strategic plan, you need to cascade that down to your teams, and then to the individual employees within each of your teams.

Every employee should have a direct line of sight of how the work they do contributes to the business achieving its goals. Without that understanding, their work may feel insignificant or irrelevant, and performance will suffer.

The strategic framework model on page 85 is a simple way to organize your thinking when devising a business strategy for your organization.

Brilliant consultancy McKinsey has created the 7S model to remind organizations of the key elements of leading a business and delivering a successful strategy. You will note that they recommend paying close attention to leadership style, the systems and structures of the business too, and show how shared values is at the heart of a high-performance organization.

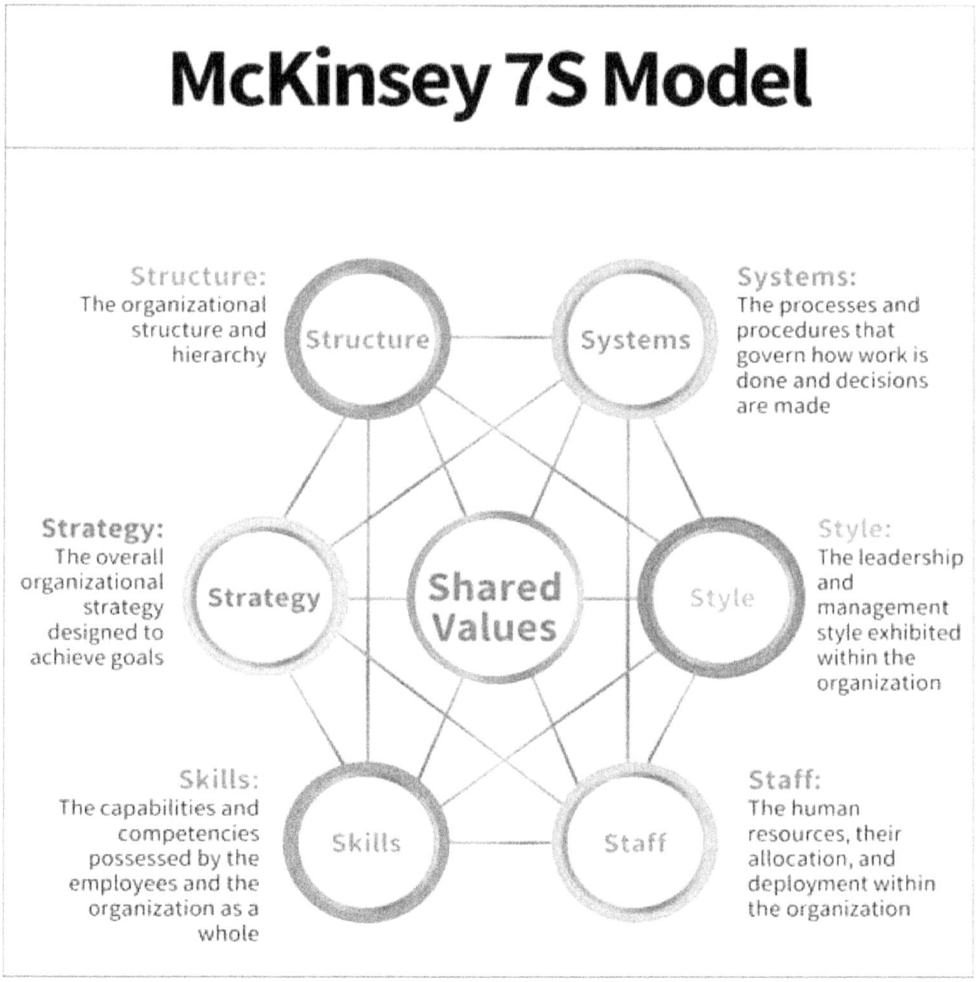

Setting Goals

Why Set Goals?

Research has shown that people respond well when they have clearly articulated goals. It gives us something to focus on and work towards, and there is profound satisfaction to be achieved from reaching our target. Without goals, we risk sleep-walking through life, or settling into a comfortable but boring routine where every day and every year feels the same. This is why companies set goals for business success, and teams have goals to promote team success and individual success, too.

What have been some of the most satisfying goals you have ever achieved (personally or professionally)?

-
-
-

And how did you feel when you achieved them?

- I felt...

How do you respond to identifying goals for your work, now?

- I respond by...

How does it feel when you achieve them?

- I feel...

How do the people in your team respond?

- They seem to feel...

Aligning Individual and Organizational Goals

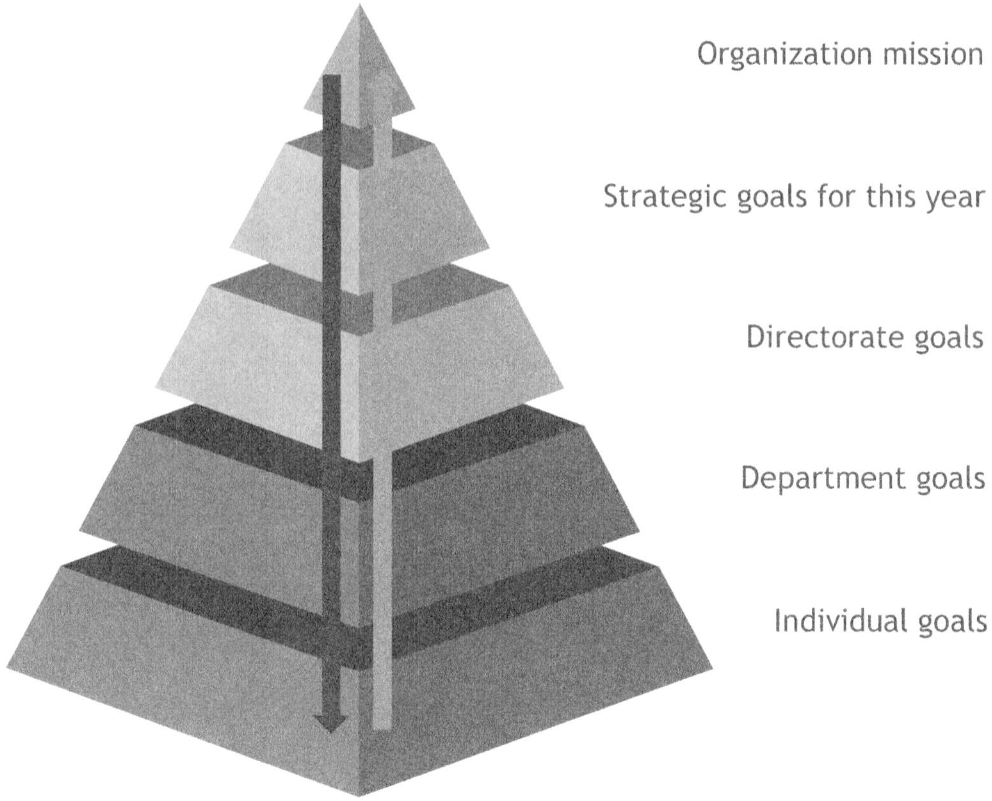

Employees need to feel that the goals you set them are meaningful. Being able to link individual goals back with department goals, and department goals with the goals for your directorate, and then with the strategic goals for this year, and ultimately to the mission of the organization... can play a powerful role in helping people to see why their work matters, and where they fit into the overall success of the enterprise.

Your job as leader is to help them feel valued as an employee, and spelling it out to them in this way will make it easier for them to understand.

How many goals should I set?

Three to five business goals and at least one professional development goal is a good number to focus performance. Many more than that, and your employee may struggle to know which to prioritize.

Updating Goals throughout the Year

As business priorities change, and our competitors change, our customers change their minds, team members come and go, some of the goals we set may become more relevant, or less so. Regular review of goals helps to ensure that an employee is focusing on the right and most relevant tasks throughout the performance cycle.

Setting SMART Goals… together

Objectives are like a road map, they help us to define where we want to go, plan the most appropriate route, check to see how close we are to our final destination and confirm that we have arrived. Without goals, we run the risk of doing the wrong things, not focusing on business priorities, and just drifting through life. That's not how businesses succeed, and neither will the employees succeed if they don't have goals of their own. The best goals are SMART goals.

Specific: Be precise when describing what you want the employee to work on. What does success look like? How will they know when they have achieved it? Rewrite this non-specific goal so that everyone understands what is expected:

"Improve product quality"

Measurable: What level of performance are you looking for? By making it measurable, both parties will know when it has been achieved. Rewrite this non-measurable goal so that everyone understands what is expected:

"Reduce customer complaints"

Agreed: the employee will not own the goal until they have agreed to work towards it. How will you ensure that they agree to the goals?

Relevant: It is not enough for the goal to be achievable; it also has to be relevant to the success of the business. How can you ensure that the employee understands the relevance of the goal you are setting them?

Time-bound: Open-ended goals are rarely achieved. Be clear about the deadline for completion of the goal. Rewrite this non-time-bound goal:

"Complete the project delivery by the end of the year."

Reviewing Progress against Goals

Setting goals is only the first step. Once you have agreed the goals, then you will need to schedule in some review time to ensure that everything is on track.

- How often should we discuss and review them?

Many companies have formalized their approach to goal setting and performance management. Even if you don't have a formal process in your organization, it will help you, your team, the organization and your career to create a culture of managing and encouraging others for high performance.

Setting clear expectations for high performance will likely be a part of your normal day to day discussions with your people anyway, but industry best practice suggests that in order to help to keep goals in the forefront of their minds, having monthly one-to-one meetings is the best way to help your people stay focused. When managing high performance, you will need to check in regularly with each person to ensure that they are still prioritizing the right things. If you can't find the time to do this on a monthly basis, at least try to do it quarterly.

Some leaders feel that because they see the people in their teams every day, they already have plenty of opportunity for a regular review. However, sometimes your people won't feel comfortable talking to you 'in passing', and would prefer some 1:1 time to discuss issues with you in private.

Scheduling in this time with each person in your team not only enables you to focus on progress against goals, but also provides an important opportunity to check in with each member of the team to find out how they are and provide clarity on business messages.

How would a regular 1:1 with each member of your team help to sustain high performance?

One-to-One (Informal) Meetings with Your Team

Research shows that the channel of communication which employees trust most is the line manager. They like to hear company messages explained, put into context, and made relevant to them so that they can build a clearer understanding of what they need to do to help the company to succeed.

Many managers take the view that 1:1 meetings with each member of their team is time-consuming and unnecessary, believing that if their staff want to talk to them about something, they would do it as part of the normal course of events. This is a mistaken belief - sometimes people feel on show if they ask for a quiet word with the boss, or see a one-to-one meeting as the place where they receive criticism.

Clear, open and honest communication is a key factor in building trust and leading a high-performance team, and should be a priority for everyone with line management responsibility. So, what should you talk about? On the next page is a suggested agenda for your one-to-one meeting, so you don't have to reinvent an agenda. You can circulate it to your team so that they know what to expect, and it gives you a logical structure to follow, so you're never stuck for things to talk about. You can take notes, or just talk. You can also schedule these meetings in advance, so everyone is clear that there are no hidden agendas.

When under-performance is an ongoing problem with a specific employee, you will need to articulate a clear performance improvement plan to help them to reach the required level of performance, spelling out exactly what changes are required, and the consequences of failing to improve. This is your job, as a leader and line manager, and they should be expecting it.

If you have discussed performance and progress at regular informal check-ins, there should be no nasty surprises for either of you.

Tip: Have your evidence to hand for when the review begins, so that you can justify your comments and observations appropriately.

How you manage the performance of people in your team will be what sets you apart as a leader.

Good performance management can transform a stressful work environment into a team spirit which is energised, motivated and optimistic about the future.

Everybody will have to have some tough conversations at some point in their career. You now have all the tools and techniques you need to prepare for and navigate those discussions.

Agenda for 1:1 Meeting

1. How's it going? - a general catch-up on current workload and responsibilities.

2. Are you enjoying the work at the moment?

3. Current priorities? - make sure your people are prioritising things which are critical to the business.

4. Any issues you're currently facing? - tells you of any problems (real or anticipated) that might affect their performance, so that together, you can formulate a plan.

5. Progress with goals - this ensures that your team are focusing their efforts in the right direction, and gives you the opportunity to refocus your employee, as well as being aware of their progress and giving them ongoing feedback. It also makes the annual appraisal much easier for both of you.

6. Recent messages - leader adds some context to company messages to ensure that they have been clearly understood, and that the employee knows what is expected of them.

7. Any feedback about my management style, or anything you need from me? This helps you to tackle any issues proactively, rather than leaving it until there is a problem.

8. Anything else you want to tell me? A final catch-all to give the employee the chance to raise personal or interpersonal issues not previously mentioned.

9. Thanks! Your opportunity to give your employee some sincere positive feedback to help them feel valued and respected.

3. Develop Productive Relationships

- Team maturity
  - Forming, storming, norming, performing
- A healthy winning culture
- Overcoming communication barriers
- Turn conflict to your advantage

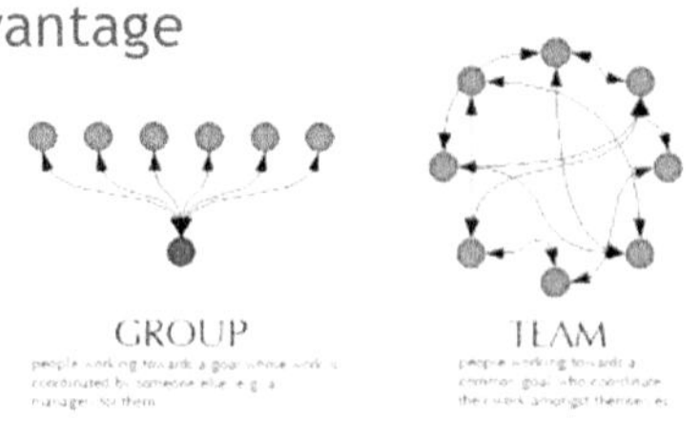

Catapult Consulting

What level of maturity is your team at right now?

What can you do to move them along towards "performing"?

Sometimes, communication barriers are as simple as being different personality types. A helpful activity to build team cohesion would be to do some profiling (MBTI or other) on the team and help them to see how they each contribute differently.

Each time there is a change to the team - someone leaves, or a new person joins you - you will likely find that the team regresses a step. Be ready to help them reconnect with the goals and with each other.

Managing Conflict

Is there a best way to handle conflict?

- Effectiveness depends on using conflict modes that fit the situation...
- ..and one situation may require a combination of approaches
- Each of us is capable of using all five modes

Catapult Consulting

What is your go-to style of navigating conflict? Does it always work for you?

Examples of Good Fit

Compete:
- Quick decisive action needed
- Important unpopular actions, i.e. cost cutting, discipline
- Vital issues when you know you are right

Collaborate:
- Concerns too important for compromise
- Gain commitment i.e. change projects
- Learn and merge insights

Compromise:
- Equal power - mutually exclusive goals i.e. union vs. management
- Expedient solutions under time pressure
- Back up to Collaborate or Compete if they fail

Avoid:
- Trivial issues
- Highly emotional issues
- No chance issues i.e. Govt Policy
- Damage of conflict outweighs benefits of resolution

Accommodate:
- When you are wrong
- When issue is more important to other than you
- When outmatched and losing
- When avoiding disruption is important

Catapult Consulting

Improving attitudes and aptitudes

Can you think of specific examples where you might need to choose a different conflict management style?

Conflict Resolution

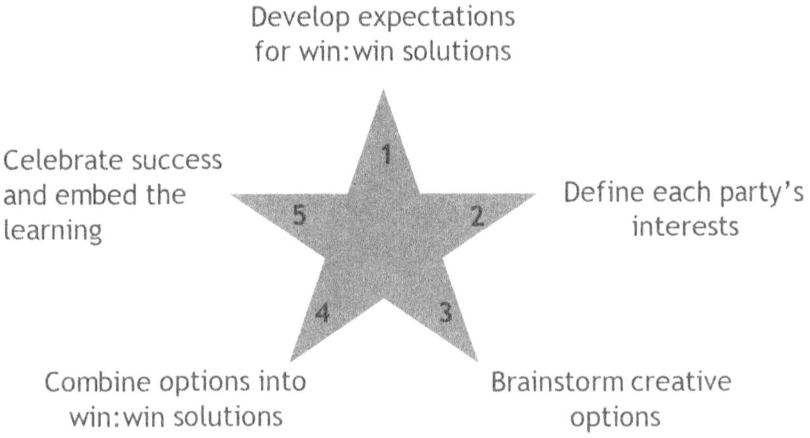

Catapult Consulting

The star model for conflict resolution suggests a five-point process to follow to resolve conflict quickly and effectively.

Intergroup Conflict

- Leader values and attitudes often shape the attitudes and behaviours of colleagues and staff
- Increasing pressure in a matrix structure
- Further communication breakdown with virtual teams
- Providing effective interpersonal relations' training contributes to stability and effective group cohesion.
- More contact between groups helps to build relationships and understanding
- Heterogeneous teams outperform homogeneous teams, and avoid Groupthink!

Catapult Consulting

Team Conflict

What issues of conflict currently exist between the different members of your leadership team?

What are you doing about it?

What issues of conflict exist between you and your team?

What are you doing about it?

What issues of conflict exist between you and other peers?

What are you doing about it?

Remember: don't jump in too soon or your team will always come to you to resolve problems instead of trying to resolve them for themselves. But also, don't leave it too long before you get involved, or relationships can suffer lasting damage.

4. Optimise the Work

- Challenge the process
- Ownership through delegation
- Clearly defined roles (play to strengths)
- Motivation
- Flexing your leadership style

- Activity: SPACE analysis

Catapult Consulting

Activity: find someone to work with and interview the other person about their strengths, priorities, aspirations, competences and experience, using the questions on the following pages.

Tip: you will need to swap books so that you have your own answers written in your own book.

SPACE Analysis

Strengths, Priorities, Aspirations, Competences, Experience

How well do you know your people?

This section will help leaders and managers to understand what drives the people they are managing. It can be used to help team members to align around a common goal or set of goals, or to create a team charter of expected behaviours and performance. It is invaluable when working to support individual career development and maintaining a healthy work life balance. You can use this form to interview each member of your team. Interviews are more effective than just getting the other person to fill in the details themselves because it helps you really understand things from their perspective.

But first, let's start with you.

Once you have answered these questions for yourself, it will be easier to understand the relevance of asking the same questions to your people.

Over the page, you will find some suggested questions for understanding motivation on a deeper level. Go through and answer them for yourself to build your self-awareness.

Employees at every level report that really enjoy the process of being asked about what's important to them. It makes them feel much more appreciated.

What are the consequences of NOT asking about strengths, priorities, aspirations, competences and experience?

STRENGTHS

Most people are very familiar with their weaknesses, having had them pointed out all through their lives. But get people talking about their strengths, and you get a powerful insight into what they do best, what they enjoy, and what makes them proud. This will help you to allocate the workload to the best people for the job.

- What are your strengths? What do you find straightforward, really easy and enjoyable to do?

- What are your particular areas of interest when you are reading books, journals or searching the net?

- Which strengths do you rely on when dealing with challenging situations?

- What are your key strengths when working with others?

- Which strengths do your colleagues admire you for?

- What feedback have you received in the past about your strengths?

PRIORITIES

Understanding an employee's personal situation will help remind you not to put undue pressure on them to work additional hours which might interfere with their other obligations.

- What is most important to you, professionally? *(Examples might include having the chance to contribute to something important, to grow in professional confidence, to build a good reputation at work)*

- What is most important to you, personally? *(Examples might include a young family, being able to get home on time, caring for a sick relative, church group or charity work)*

ASPIRATIONS

Aspirations are very personal and an important source of motivation. If you know what an employee wants for the future, you can help them to work towards it.

What are your aspirations...

- Professionally? *(Examples might include getting promoted, achieving professional qualifications, high profile projects, working with experts, being mentored by someone senior)*

- Personally? *(Examples might include success in a chosen sporting league, to start a charitable foundation or raise funds for a charity, to get published or develop a singing career)*

- Where do you see yourself in five years' time? *(examples might include a senior role, going self employed, winning an industry award for contribution, or pursuing further academic study)*

COMPETENCES

Competences may be a source of capability for you to tap into, but don't overload someone with these tasks, especially if they don't enjoy them very much.

Even if you don't particularly enjoy doing it, in which areas or tasks have you learnt to become really competent?

- Professionally? *(Examples might include project planning, understanding a piece of legislation, or speaking at an industry event)*

- Personally? (*Examples might include resolving conflict at work, mediation skills, becoming a mental health first aider)*

- What have you learnt to be good at, but actually don't enjoy at all? *(Examples might include copy checking, creating a knowledge database, resolving difficult customer complaints)*

EXPERIENCE

If you didn't interview this employee, you may not be aware of previous experience they have which could be really relevant to an upcoming project.

- Outline your main professional background and experience

- Which work experiences and challenges have given you the greatest satisfaction?

- Which non-work experiences have you enjoyed most?

- What do you like doing in your spare time?

- Which community activities do you support (if any)?

5. Protect the Team

- Dealing with outside influences
- Guarding the team from itself
- Guarding the team from YOUrself
- Managing diverse stakeholders
- Balancing project constraints
- Identifying 'Groupthink'

Catapult Consulting

Why might you need to protect the team from yourself?

In what circumstances would Groupthink be a problem for your team?

6. Sustain Peak Performance

- Co-located vs dispersed teams
- Heterogeneous vs homogeneous
- Hard work into enjoyable experience
- Recognising success
- Personal accountability
- Lessons learned
- Autonomy

Catapult Consulting

Giving people autonomy is proven to be highly motivating. Autonomy works when all employees have a clear understanding of the goal. Once they understand the 'what', you can give them more freedom to decide the 'how'.

Alignment and Autonomy

Catapult Consulting

How much autonomy do you currently give your people?

How could you go about giving them greater autonomy?

Motivation and Engagement

To understand motivation, you need to understand expectations.

Our unwritten expectations may not form part of a formal written employment contract, but we are expecting certain things anyway, and assume that the company is expecting to deliver those things.

This is called a psychological contract.

Psychological Contract

Unspoken, implicit agreement between employee and organisation that each party will fulfil their obligations and duties towards the other.

May involve assumptions that the organisation is no longer able (or willing) to fulfill... with profound consequences.

Catapult Consulting

What expectations did you have about your career / employer before you joined?

With hindsight, how realistic were they?

What unrealistic expectations might exist within your team?

How do you want to address that, without demotivating them?

Dominic Cadbury said "There is no such thing as a career path anymore; there is only crazy-paving, and you have to lay that yourself."

How might this apply to new starters?

Motivation: The Key to High Performance Culture

Motivation has been the subject of thousands of research projects. When we can understand what really interests another person, we can work out how to get the best out of them. This is crucial when driving the performance of individual team members at work. And performance management means managing and sustaining good performance, as well as challenging poor performance.

If you ask somebody why they go to work, they will probably mention all the usual look-good **extrinsic motivators** first:

- Salary, benefits, bonus, promotion, status, grade rise, winning, recognition.

But if you start to dig a little deeper, people start to mention other things, the feel-good **intrinsic motivators**:

- Social interaction, learning and growth, to apply their knowledge, to have fun, for self-expression, to fulfil a sense of purpose, and to make a difference.

Recognition will likely appear in both of these lists, but HOW people like to be recognised for good performance will depend on their personality type and their career and personal priorities.

Fact: Most people will claim that they come to work for the money. In fact, money is only part of the motive - it's much more about what money will enable them to do. There is no doubt that the less money someone earns, the more important money will be to them. But research into high performing sports professionals and corporate professionals alike has shown that people who are intrinsically motivated (to be the very best performer they can be, to achieve their personal best, to contribute to a successful team, and to represent their business, team or country) generally outperform those people who are more interested in fees, bonuses and celebrity parties.

What Motivates YOU?

Let's start by thinking about what really motivates YOU to come to work, and do this job. You might just surprise yourself.

In the table below, there is a list of the common reasons people mention about why they come to work. Take a few minutes now to complete this activity. Compare each reason (starting with A) with each of the other reasons (B, C, D...L) and put a line in the score column. So, when comparing reason A with reason B, if reason A is more important to you, put a mark in the score column against A. Then compare A and C. If C is more important, put a mark against C. Compare reason A with all the other reasons in turn. Then do the same with B, comparing with each of the other reasons. The last paired comparison will be K vs L.

Put a ✓ in the corresponding box each time you select one option over another. Add them up once you have compared each item with each of the others.

	Reason	Your Score ✓
A	Money (lifestyle, provide for family etc)	
B	To learn and grow	
C	For the social interaction	
D	To do interesting work	
E	To get out of the house	
F	Because daytime TV is rubbish	
G	I like working	
H	To set a good example to my kids	
I	To use my education and skills	
J	To get promoted	
K	To be a good citizen	
L	To make a difference	

Well, was it what you first thought?

What were your top three?

People are not all motivated the same, and we do well not to make assumptions. When you can reward high performance with something that really matters to an employee, they will likely feel even more motivated.

Do this exercise with your team members to find out what really drives them.

Making the Grade

- Why people come to work
- Extrinsic v intrinsic motivators
- Why some people fail
- Performance attitudes
- Confidence -> competence
- Team dynamics
- Understanding the consequences of failure
- Positive intention

Catapult Consulting

All of the above can have a significant impact on levels of motivation at work.

Understanding Motivation

Theory X

Employees:

- Avoid work where possible
- Refuse to take responsibility / accountability
- Have extrinsic motivation only and respond to reward / status

Managers:

- Expect low performance
- Must drive employees and manage them closely
- Distrust people and dictate decisions
- Find negative motivators (threats) to be most effective

Theory Y

Employees:

- Enjoy work and pursue it
- Are responsible and accountable
- Have intrinsic motivation and respond to leadership

Managers:

- Expect high performance
- Lead and macro-manage
- Trust staff and facilitate decision-making
- Use positive motivators
- Celebrate group success

Autocracy ▲ **Democracy**

Catapult Consulting

In addition to Theory X and Theory Y, there is also a Theory Z, which suggests that depending on the individual, you might need a combination of both X and Y.

Who might that approach work best for?

Maslow's Hierarchy of Needs

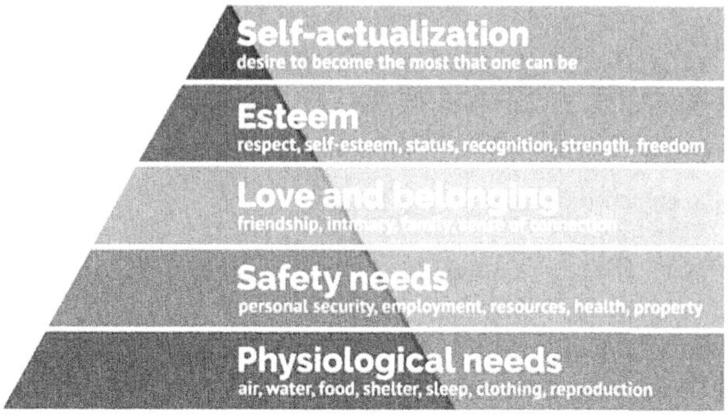

Maslow's hierarchy of needs is a simple but profound way to understand what people need in their lives. Once you get past the lower order needs - food, water, shelter, safety - people will start to look for a sense of belonging, to feel good about themselves and to find personal meaning and a sense of accomplishment in their work.

Herzberg: Hygiene Factors

Herzberg argued that some of the things we think will actively motivate others, only serve to meet basic needs. The factors on the bottom row are not motivators in their own right, but they are demotivators if they are not present, or not working well. The factors on the top row are what really drive motivation, and they are intrinsic (feel-good) factors.

High Employee Engagement Leads to High Performance

Global research company, Gallup, specialize in measuring employee engagement at work. They have identified 12 questions - usually included as part of an employee satisfaction survey - as the key drivers of employee engagement. In other words, if an employee scores highly on each of these 12 questions, they are more likely to stay and work hard for their employer.

According to the Gallup research, around a third of staff report feeling actively disengaged at work. A further third report feeling neither engaged nor disengaged, in other words, sometimes they feel engaged, sometimes they don't. This means that only a third (at best) report feeling actively engaged at work. These people are the only ones really working at their best, and helping their organization to succeed.

If you are looking at your to-do list and worrying that you don't have enough people in your team to get the job done properly, the reality is probably more that you don't have sufficiently engaged people in your team, or if you do, that they are not prioritizing effectively, or that issues of underperformance are going unchallenged because you are too busy to do anything about it. The higher the levels of engagement, the better the performance, and the more manageable the workload.

The good news is that you can do something about all of that.

Have a look at the 12 points on the next page, and give yourself a score out of 10 to reflect your own experience at work.

It should be easy, but leaders don't always make time for the most important elements, such as providing recognition for good performance (Q4), encouraging individual development (Q6), or explaining the significance of the work they do (Q8).

How Engaged are YOU?

How would you score yourself (out of 10) against each of the Gallup Q12 elements of engagement? And would the people in your team score the same? As a leader, if you are not highly engaged, you will struggle to inspire your people.

Nr	Element	Your score (out of 10)
1	I know what is expected of me at work	
2	I have the equipment I need to do my job	
3	I have the opportunity to do what I do best, every day at work	
4	In the last week, I have received recognition for working well	
5	Someone at work seems to care about me as a person	
6	Someone at work encourages my development	
7	At work, I feel that my opinions count	
8	The mission of my organization makes me feel that my work is important	
9	My colleagues are committed to doing quality work	
10	I have a close friend at work	
11	In the last 6 months, someone has discussed my progress with me	
12	This last year, I have had opportunities at work to learn and grow	

There is a lot more information on the Gallup website, and their various publications explain in much more detail how you can use their research to create a high-performance organizational culture.

Drivers of Employee Engagement

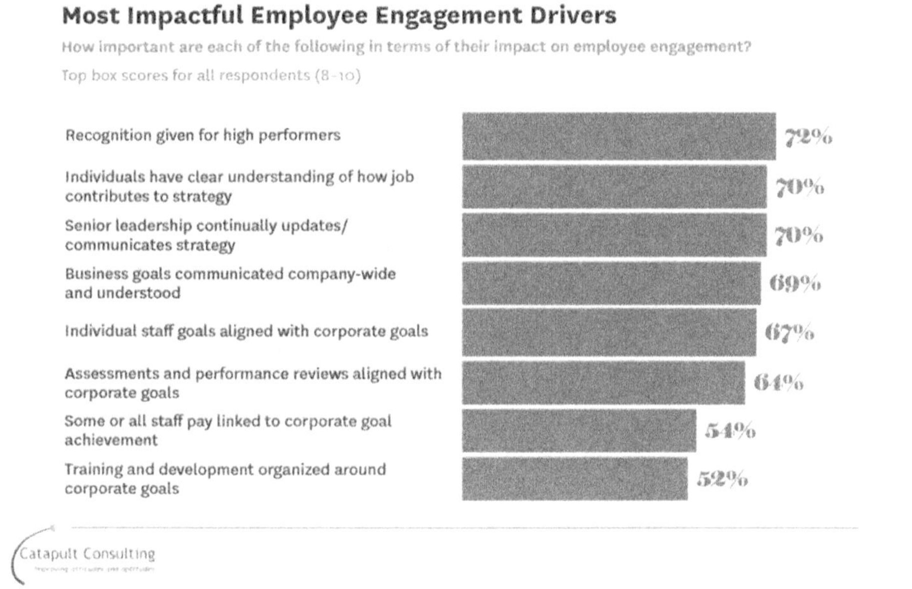

Employee Engagement Action Plan

Take a few moments to reflect upon the key drivers of employee engagement, and think about how you can raise engagement in your team.

Did you notice how many of the key drivers mention understanding of and alignment with the link with the business goals? Strategic alignment is CRUCIAL to an organization's success.

What do you already do well?

What do you need to prioritise?

What action will you take to resolve this?

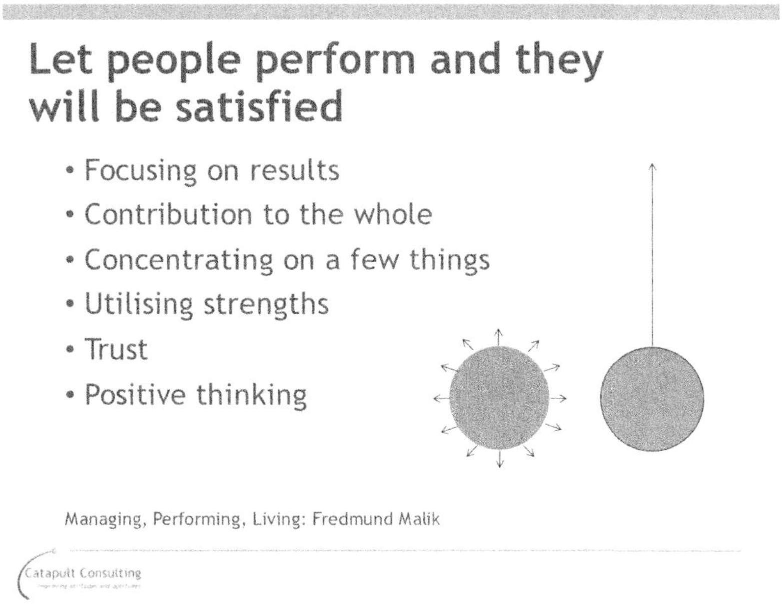

When you lead your people effectively, creating a clear sense of direction and helping them to understand the part they play, you end up with everyone pulling in the same direction. With good leadership, your people will be able to move one meter in a single direction, instead of 1cm in 100 different directions.

Talent Management

- You get the people you deserve!
- Nurturing the heir apparent: good talent management ensures that you retain good people and knowledge
- Courage and consideration: we must be honest with our people about their performance and career prospects
- Letting the right one in: are our recruitment processes delivering the people we need?
- Who am I being?

Catapult Consulting

You get the people you deserve: discuss.

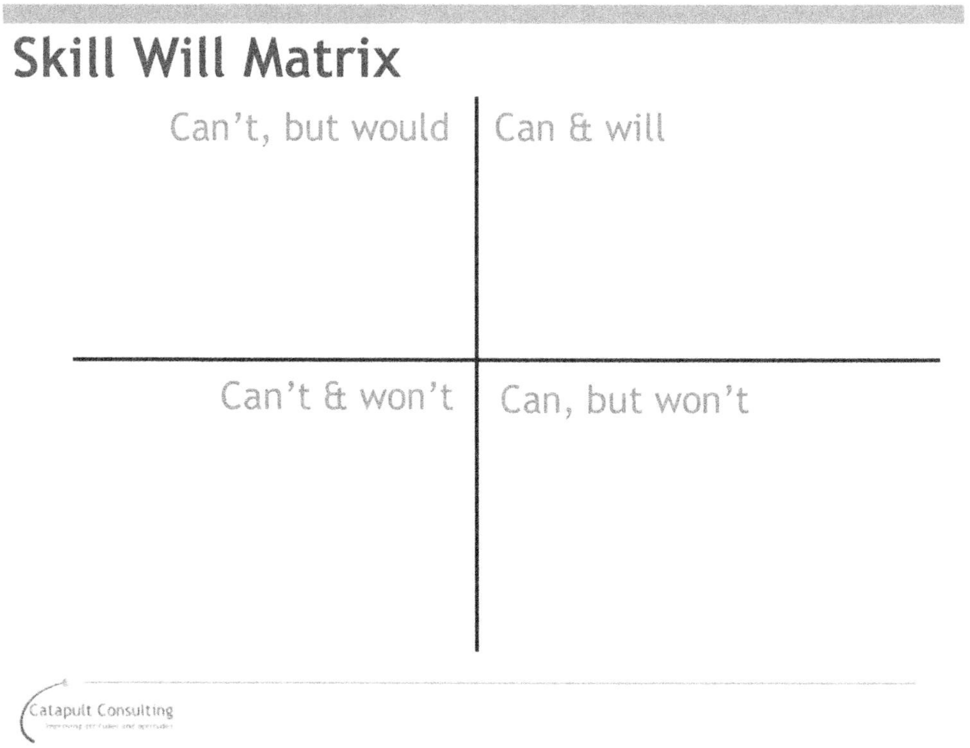

Sometimes, despite all the support we give them, our employees just don't perform as well as we expected. There is a number of possible reasons for that:

- They don't like the work
- They cannot do the work
- They have problems outside of work
- They don't have a good relationship with their co-workers
- They don't have a good relationship with their line manager
- They don't understand the significance / relevance of the work
- The work doesn't play to their strengths
- They are disengaged, bored, or looking for another job

The Skill Will matrix acknowledges the different attitudes that you might observe from people in your team. Knowing where they are on this grid can give you a really helpful steer on how to manage them in a way that best suits their development needs and encourages them to do their very best.

Thinking about each person in your team… which quadrant best describes their current performance and attitude?

How are you shaping that?

In which quadrant does <u>your</u> name belong?

What are your strategies for managing performance in each quadrant?

Can & Will: Do

Can & Will: Don't

Can but Won't: Do

Can but Won't: Don't

Can't but Would: Do

Can't but Would: Don't

Can't and Won't: Do

Can't and Won't: Don't

Nothing damages performance more than when good performers watch you tolerate poor performers, so examine what you tolerate.

Managing Performance

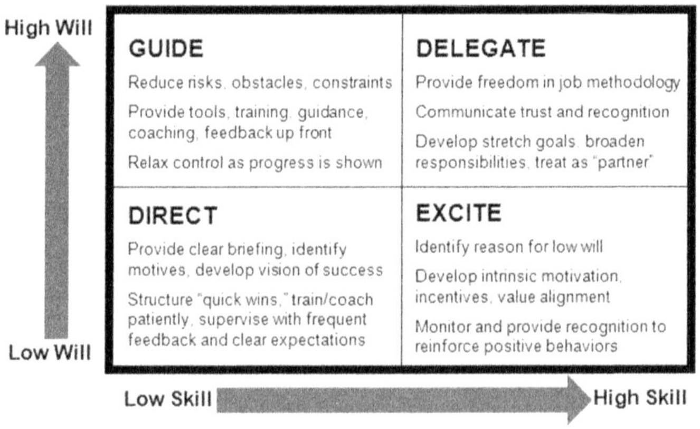

Is everybody in your team performing at the right level?

Devise a plan to raise performance for each person in your team:

Remember: addressing issues of performance and attitude is YOUR job, not HR's.

Crucible Conversations™

A Crucible Conversation may involve giving or receiving some difficult development feedback.

Delivered badly, difficult feedback can lead to disengagement

Delivered well, it can lead to a huge developmental leap forward!

Have the backbone to give it and to take it

Maintain absolute respect at all times

Helping to resolve and redirect, not punish

Focus on common goals

Having (rather than avoiding) difficult discussions is key to sustaining high performance

Catapult Consulting

Define Your Outcomes Carefully

- Think

  What will people think / know / understand as a result of the meeting?

- Feel

  How will people feel? Confident? Satisfied? Empowered?

- Do

  What will the employee do as a result?

Catapult Consulting

Think of a Crucible Conversation you need to have with a colleague. How will you prepare for it?

What do you want the other person to think, feel, and DO differently as a result of the conversation?

Framework for Crucible Conversations™

- Outline the situation / performance (evidence)
- Express your feelings about the situation (NOT the person)
- Explain that this is something that needs to be addressed effectively, for everyone's sake
- Invite the other person to comment
- Validate their feelings
- Discuss what needs to happen
- Agree a set of next steps
- Review for effectiveness

Catapult Consulting

People report feeling anxious about having Crucible Conversations with others. The answer to this is to practise, practise, practise! You can rehearse this structure when you are driving, or waiting in line, or drinking coffee. When you have practised, you will be reciting what you have already learned, rather than trying to find the right words for the first time.

Checking in on your own Unconscious Bias

We all make snap judgements about people, and form opinions through our own filters on the world. It's hard (but not impossible) to update those filters, and judge others as kindly as we hope they will judge us. But we really need to be mindful of these filters, or biases, especially when it comes to measuring and managing the performance of our people.

Have you ever met someone for the first time, and immediately liked them? This is called the halo effect, or affinity bias, and is usually because they remind you of someone else you know and like. It will influence your feelings and opinions of them every time you meet them or work with them.

But have you ever had that experience where on meeting someone for the first time, you take an instant dislike to them? That's called the horn effect. Again, it's usually because subconsciously, they remind you of someone else. The problem is that we then treat them as someone we don't like, and that will affect every single discussion with them.

Either way, whether or not you like somebody, it will be subtly communicated in every subsequent interaction - the warmth of your smile, the attention you pay, your body language, the words you use, what you say about them to others, and the feedback you give them. And if you know that someone doesn't like you (no matter how well they try and hide it), you will sense it, and will tend to be less willing to help, less forgiving of their mistakes, less complimentary when talking about them, and generally be less cooperative when working with them.

Worse still, if we have made a snap judgement about someone (and we all do it), they will have to work extra hard to change that judgement, because we tend only to notice information that confirms the judgement we have already made. That is called confirmation bias.

As leaders, we will undoubtedly have opinions about each person in our team. It's called observer bias. But are those opinions fair, or are we making judgements through the filter of our own biases?

For example, is this employee's attention to detail *really* disastrous, or is it just that they made a mistake recently, and it has affected our judgement of them.

- Beware of recency bias, where we recall only a recent example or incident, and make that the whole story about someone's capability.

Is this person's attention to detail *really* poor, or is it just that YOU have excellent attention to detail, whereas the other person is more of a 'big picture' thinker?

- Be aware of in-group bias, where we tend to treat people more favourably when they are like us.

Is this person really an under-performer, or is it that you just don't like them?

Finding the Right Words

Leaders and managers may avoid having difficult conversations at work for a number of reasons. Often, they are not sure of their facts, and are afraid to make unfounded accusations. If this applies to you, the simple answer is to do your homework in advance of a conversation, and have your evidence to hand.

Some managers doubt the legitimacy of their complaint, and wonder if maybe they should have already fixed the problem themselves. But as a leader, you will not have time to do all the work yourself; you will need to rely on the people in your team, and not only is it your right to challenge your staff, they will be expecting it of you, because you are the leader, and they will come to lose respect for you if you don't.

The main reason that managers avoid having the difficult conversations about performance at work is that they are afraid the other person will take the criticism badly, and the situation will quickly escalate, resulting in an argument or accusations of bullying and harassment.

No matter how thorny the subject, knowing the right words to say will help you to navigate such a conversation with professionalism and poise, and is less likely to end up in a difficult conversation with HR.

Dealing with Emotional Outbursts

When faced with the evidence of poor performance, unacceptable behavior, undesirable attitudes or inconsistent attendance, some people will quickly become angry or tearful. It's a defence mechanism, designed to make the problem go away, and incredibly, will probably stem from some early childhood conditioning. The point at which a parent gives into their child's demands is the point at which the child learns how to get their own way; if crying makes the parent give in to the demand for sweets, then the child learns to cry to get what they want. If having a huge tantrum is what finally makes the parent relent, the child learns that tantrums are a quicker way to get their needs met. Children are not master-manipulators; they are just trying to figure out what will work. Incredibly, then, those same childhood techniques which worked so well when they were young may have unwittingly become their go-to tactic for dealing with things that feel outside of their control. One thing is very likely: if the other person is shouting or if they are crying, it will almost certainly be a mask for fear. Fear is a hugely compelling emotion, and can lead to sudden and unexpected outbursts. Whilst it may feel like an uphill struggle dealing with an employee who seems to revert to tears when the going gets tough, this section will help you to stop rewarding that behaviour, and to make sure you stay in control of the situation. A shouting employee can feel hugely intimidating, but in truth, it is extremely unlikely that they will resort to a physical attack because that would seal their fate and pretty much guarantee termination of contract. Again, this section outlines words to use which will de-escalate a heated discussion in a way that takes the heat out of the situation without a power struggle.

1. Deal with the emotion, first. When someone is shouting or crying at you, this is their raw response to their discomfort. Until you acknowledge that emotional response, you will not be able to move past it. One thing is for sure: the words 'CALM DOWN' will never serve you, here; nobody was ever calmer as a result of being told to calm down. You can strike those words from your vocabulary - they will not help. Likewise, don't enter into an argument with the other person, because they may be much better at arguing than you; either way, you lose all credibility. Your job is not to win the fight, but to reason with the other person to improve their performance or behaviour. An escalating argument is a sign you no longer hold the power, and that makes it much harder for you to resolve.

2. "I can see you are very angry." Use these words when the other person is raising their voice and becoming angry. Don't say "I can see you are very upset" if they are showing anger because they are likely to correct you in the strongest words possible. Tone of voice is all important here, too. If you sound patronising or condescending, it is likely to add fuel to flames. If your tone is dismissive or accompanied by eye-rolling, the other person will likely feel insulted, and again, the flames grow higher. Instead, maintain calm, adult-to-adult eye contact, and state clearly that you can see they are angry. A fairly deadpan delivery of the line can help. This tells them, yep, I get it; you're angry. It's usually enough to make them stop a moment, especially if this is a new tactic from you.

   If the difficult conversation is one that has prompted tears from the other person, then the process is the same, except you would substitute the words "I can see you are very upset" and possibly use a slightly softer tone, and don't be patronising. If the other person thinks they have provoked you and you are now responding in a very soft and gentle way, backing down to de-escalate, it may reinforce their behavior, and continue to be their go-to response when conversations become uncomfortable. Again, however, don't get drawn into their drama.

3. "Perhaps in your position, I might feel the same."
   When you say this, they hear "You're right to feel that way" ... except that that wasn't what you said. But they feel validated, and having our frustrations validated is one of the most powerful and emotionally intelligent ways to manage a situation like this. Once you have landed this line, pause a moment so that they can take stock.

4. "Help me to understand what's going on for you."
   This gives the other person their chance to speak, to vent, and to list out everything that is prompting this emotional response. Just listen, without interrupting, and without passing judgement. This is their drama; it's not for you to decide - at this point - if their frustrations are justified. Note, when you use the word 'why?' you are telling the other person to justify themselves. The words "help me to understand" is much less provocative.

5. Make a list.
   If they mention it, write it down into a list, to show that you are listening, and also to help you work through and address each of their frustrations in turn.

6. Read it back to them.
   Again, this demonstrates that you were listening. Once you have reached the end, ask, "Did I miss anything out?" This carries a different weight to "Is that all?" which sounds dismissive. If they mention anything else, add it in, then read the list out again.

7. "Let's see what we can do about each of these things, now."

   Once you have been through this process, it will usually have taken all the heat out of their anger, and will enable you both to proceed with a discussion on how to move forward. Go through each item on their list, being clear about which things you can influence, and which ones you can't. Sometimes you discover that the main reasons for the other person's frustrations lie with things entirely outside of your or their control, and sometimes are things which have nothing to do with work anyway. Redirecting them to an employee assistance scheme, or gently suggesting that maybe other professional support (such as a coach, a therapist, or other advisory service) might be their best option, will save you from getting embroiled in their personal situation. Even though you may want to help, it will make managing their poor performance much more difficult for you if you start getting involved.

8. Agree what it is in your control (as leader), and make notes on what steps you will take. You can email your commitment to the employee, so that they know exactly what to expect from you. Then do it; be true to your word.

9. Agree what action they need to take. If they haven't brought a pen and notepad, find one for them, and ask them to make some notes. If they tell you they don't need to, and that they will remember, ask them to make notes anyway. Once they have their notes, ask them to read their notes back to you so that you can be sure they have understood what they need to do. Then ask them to go back to their desk and send you an email, listing out their actions. DO NOT do that part for them. Don't give them a copy of your notes, either, and don't send the email with the list of actions. Until they write them down and commit in writing, they won't own those actions, and can easily deny the discussion at a future date. If the email they send only lists some of the actions, ask them to write a new email to you containing the full list of actions.

10. Thank them. When you are able to end your meeting on a positive note, shaking hands, warm smile, they feel reassured that no matter how uncomfortable the conversation has been, you have treated them fairly and with respect, and they are much more likely to engage in a positive way in future conversations.

When the other person sees that instead of backing down, you stick with the conversation until it has reached a conclusion, they will stop relying on that strong emotional response, and those conversations will become much, much easier in future.

What if the problem gets worse?

In the unlikely event that the words above don't bring the situation back under your control, and instead, the other person raises their voice, getting more and more irate, maybe shouting, gesticulating, and threatening you, you still have options which don't result in you losing your nerve, or losing any teeth.

"Oh, that's interesting..."

This one will likely come as a surprise, and will make them stop to hear what you are going to say next. Pause a moment to let your words sink in. Initially, they may feel justified in their outburst. Then you follow up with this:

"Why would you think it's OK to speak to me like that?"

Delivered in a cold, calm and emotionally deadpan way, the two parts of this response will usually completely disarm the most furious employee.

"I am trying to help you to resolve this situation, and you appear not to want to do the same. We can do this informally, right now, or we can make it formal, and involve HR, which will go on your employee record. Tell me right now which outcome you want."

Specific Situations

Austrian doctor and family therapist Alfred Adler argued that you should never need to tell off a child without using the opportunity to enhance their self-esteem at the same time. Some parents do this brilliantly well: "Johnny, that was a really unkind thing you did there. What happened? That's not like you! You are a kind and wonderfully thoughtful child, who is much better than that. What will you do differently next time?"

There are some other words you might like to practise saying when preparing for a difficult conversation, covering a wide range of awkward topics. Let's see how using the language of positive assumptions can help to make a difficult conversation easier.

- Body Odour

"This is awkward, so I'm just going to get straight to the point. Your clothes don't smell very fresh. I have no doubt that you shower regularly, and that your personal hygiene is good, but I suspect that your laundry detergent isn't up to the job. Can I recommend that this weekend, you put all your work clothes through a hot wash with a biological detergent, and send any non-machine washable items to the dry cleaners. You might even want to nip into town and buy a couple of new shirts. How you smell doesn't affect your competence, but it does affect (and is affecting) how comfortable others feel working with you, and as a valued member of this team, I cannot allow that to become a problem."

- Timekeeping

"Looking at the clocking-in data, I notice that you have been late into work a few times recently. I know you to be a very committed and professional colleague, and that's not like you at all. Is there something we need to talk about? Let's get this sorted - I would hate for other people to draw the wrong conclusions about your commitment."

- Good performance, poor attitude / behaviour

"Let's discuss your recent performance on XYZ project. I know that this is a real area of expertise and I am delighted to have you on the team. Getting the job done well is crucial to the success of this project, and I have no concerns whatsoever about what you have achieved. But we need to discuss how you go about achieving it. I am hearing several reports about late submissions, process workarounds which breach our regulatory obligations, and abrupt and discourteous customer service. This absolutely cannot continue. People's memories are poor - they won't remember that you did a good job, they will only remember that you came across as rude or unprofessional, and that will end up hurting your career."

- Poor Performance

"Let's discuss this report that you have kindly pulled together. Here are the things that I really like about it; its strong points, good grammar and excellent structure. But some of this data looks a bit shaky, and I think we have more up to date information available for this section here. In addition, whilst the first three parts are well written, the recommendations section - where you can add most value - is a bit light, and doesn't reflect your expertise. In summary, this report isn't bad, and if I had received it from anyone else in the business, I might think it was good enough. But I know you are capable of much better work than this, and I want you to take it away and rework the sections we have discussed to ensure that this is the very best example of what you are capable of."

- Poor performance, poor attitude

"We need to sit down and properly evaluate some of the challenges you are facing right now. Once upon a time, you were the very best of all the candidates we interviewed, and that's why we offered you the job. With all your years of knowledge and experience, we should be seeing much better performance from you. Help me to understand what's going on for you?"

Note: Everybody is brilliant at something, and this person might simply be in the wrong job. Take care not to be too judgemental - it may have been a management oversight to place this employee in their current role.

"I think it would be really useful for us to go back and maybe do some strengths assessments and personality profiling with you. I know you'll be brilliant at something, and I am just wondering if this role isn't the best fit for you."

- Broken Promises

"At our meeting on (date), you agreed to complete a series of actions designed to address the performance issues we have been discussing. Despite that reassurance, I am not seeing any progress. I will fight to keep you in my team as long as I continue to believe that you are a strong and capable contributor. But you need to help me. I want you to go back to your desk right now, and send me an email listing all the actions we have agreed, and stating your commitment to complete them ahead of our next review meeting, which will be at the same time next week. I need you to understand that if you don't complete those actions, I will begin a formal performance improvement process with you, as laid out in our HR policy."

When you ask an employee to email you written confirmation of the actions they have agreed to take, you have a signed commitment to do the work. That way, if they still don't complete their actions, they have then broken their own promises. This is the point at which you involve someone from your Human Resources team, and begin a formal performance improvement process (often referred to as a PIP).

Note: if you begin a formal performance improvement process (i.e., which could lead to termination of employment), you will need to take detailed and accurate notes for your records. Do it while the conversation is still fresh in your mind, in case their version of events differs wildly from yours.

Do you need to have some crucible conversations at work?

Who with?

How will you plan for the discussion:

> What do you want the other person to think, feel and do differently as a result of the Crucible Conversation?
>
> What evidence will you need to gather?
>
> When will you have the conversation?

How will you stay in control if the discussion gets heated?

How will you close the conversation?

How will you follow up?

Leader as Coach

- How much coaching do you do in your day job?
- Rate your current coaching ability?
- Where do you want to focus your improvement efforts?
- Self assessment activity

Catapult Consulting

Coaching Self Assessment

Commitment to professional development	Commitment to performance improvement	Assessment, diagnosis & planning	Face to face feedback	Attention	Listening & responding	Implementation & follow up
10	10	10	10	10	10	10
9	9	9	9	9	9	9
8	8	8	8	8	8	8
7	7	7	7	7	7	7
6	6	6	6	6	6	6
5	5	5	5	5	5	5
4	4	4	4	4	4	4
3	3	3	3	3	3	3
2	2	2	2	2	2	2
1	1	1	1	1	1	1

Catapult Consulting

Which coaching competences are strongest for you?

Where is your greatest development opportunity?

GROW Model of Coaching

Goal	What do you want? What will that get you? What is exciting about this goal? What's even more important than this goal? How will you measure the results? What does success look like? What's the big picture?
Reality	How are things going right now? How do you feel? What values and needs are most important? What is the biggest concern? What resources are available? What barriers do you face? What does the resistance really mean?
Options	What are some of the ways you could approach this issue? Would you like to brainstorm some options? In your wildest dreams, what strategies would you choose? If you had more money, time or authority, what would you do? What if you could start all over? What are some of the advantages and disadvantages of each option?
Way Forward	Which option is your best choice? When will you get started? What's the first step? What else do you need to do? On a scale of 1-10, how committed are you to this plan? What would take you to a ten? What accountability structures would support you? How will you celebrate success?

Catapult Consulting

Don't 'Tell', COACH!

- Human nature to consider own interests first
  - What is the other person trying to protect?
- Make positive assumptions
- Appeal to the nobler motives
- Keep asking questions, not giving answers
  - "What would that give you?"
  - "So what do you want to do about that?"
- Appreciative enquiry: ask what is already working well, and what they want to build on, using their strengths
- Ask: Will it help you to reach your goal?

Catapult Consulting

Coaching as a Leadership Practice

Coaching is being used by more and businesses as the single most effective way to get an employee to accept and own personal goals and plans for improvement. It can be used to reinforce training and company messages (such as health & safety) and is at its most effective when the coaching asks enough questions to help the person being coached to come up with all the answers themselves.

The coaching process tends to follow this 6-point structure:

1. Accepting/outlining the challenge
2. Determine immediate actions that give most value
3. Agreeing actions
4. First step commitment
5. Planned activity
6. Deadline & feedback

Using a coaching style of management involves doing a lot more asking than telling. The people in your teams are usually the best placed to know how to resolve the issues they are facing, but they do not always have confidence in their own ideas.

By adopting an 'Ask' rather than 'Tell' style, a coaching leader will encourage more of a pull approach as opposed to push.

Which is your default style? Is it helping your team to think for themselves?

How could a coaching style of management help to improve their performance?

Don't Jump into 'Solutions' Mode.

When a leader tells an employee the solution to a problem - instead of coaching them to find their own solution - there are a number of possible consequences.

How many can you identify?

Remember: People are much more committed to their own ideas.

Attitudes to Coaching

In order for coaching to be really effective, the other person needs to have the right attitude towards being coached. Take a moment to reflect on the people in your team. How would you describe their...?

- **Willingness to learn?**
- **Openness to feedback?**
- **Understanding of the process?**
- **Desire to change performance or behaviour?**
- **Ability to be honest (with themselves, as well as with you)?**

Ready for Coaching?

When the person in your team is ready and willing and interested in how coaching can help them to raise their game, they will see coaching as an opportunity to improve and exceed expectations. However, you may find on occasions that somebody is really good at seeming to agree with the need for change, but never actually gets around to implementing the actions and improvements you have discussed. They may be very good at giving excuses or saying that everything is fine now. Watch out for 'smoke screen' language / behaviour... it is often a sign of some defensiveness or fear about what is expected of them.

If coaching fails to improve performance, it could be for a number of reasons, such as the following:

- Leader fails to make enough time to coach
- Goals were not clearly defined at the start
- The coaching leader tries to solve the issue for them, leading to lack of ownership
- Milestones missed
- Lack of rapport between coaching leader and employee
- Lack of commitment by employee
- Lack of honesty by employee
- Other reasons?
-
-
-

Tip: Always be clear with an employee as to why you believe coaching to be a good idea. If they trust your motives, they are more likely to engage in the process.

Coaching with the GROW model

When reviewing performance with an employee, it can be easy just to focus on what is missing or incomplete, asking questions such as “What’s the problem here?” or “Why are you still missing this goal?”. But that can be very demotivating. We cannot afford to let poor performance go unchallenged, however there are more effective ways to focus on it. That’s where coaching comes in.

Coaching enables us to help our people work out ways to achieve their personal performance goals and to come up with their own solutions to the challenges presented.

In order not to get bogged down in the detail, it helps to have a structure to follow when discussing how a team member can work to achieve their goals.

John Whitmore wrote a book called “Coaching for Performance” and this is used by coaches all over the world to help them structure a good coaching dialogue aimed at sustaining a high-performance organization. In his book, Whitmore introduces the ‘GROW’ model for coaching; giving coaches a logical flow to their discussions. GROW stands for Goal, Reality, Options, Will. He recommends asking questions in this order to help our people think about their goal in a logical way, shaping and structuring their thought process to come up with ideas on how to achieve them.

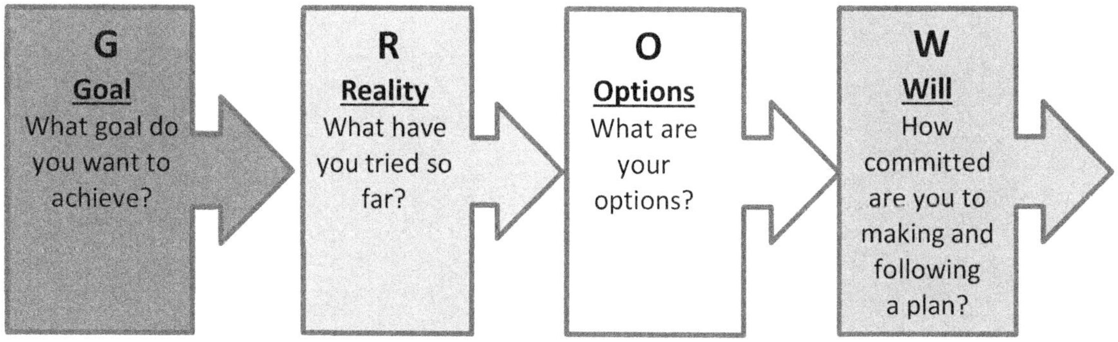

If you want to GROW your people,

you can see why SPACE is so important.

A Coaching Style of Leadership

Coaching is a great way to help an employee to come up with their own solutions to a problem, and people are much more committed to seeing their own ideas succeed.

Besides, if every member of your team has learned not to think for themselves, but always to ask you, how will you ever find time for all the other elements of your role?

There are many well qualified and very experienced business coaches offering their services. But you don't need to be a qualified coach in order to use a coaching style of management. Perhaps you have worked with one already.

On the following page, there is a list of common coaching questions which will help to get you started.

This list is by no means exhaustive, and you will be able to think of other questions for each stage that would help build focus and drive. Over time, you will hear or think of other good questions to add to the list and make it truly personal. In the meantime, you can simply use it as a quick reference guide to help you to get started.

Coaching Questions

Goal

What exactly do you want to achieve?
How measurable is that?
How will you know when you've achieved it?
By when do you want to do it?
To what extent is it within your control?
Is it positive, desirable and challenging enough for you?
If you could have it, would you truly want it?

Reality

What have you achieved so far in reaching this goal?
What have you learnt from that?
Could you break it down into more manageable sub-goals?
Who else do you need to help you reach your goal?
Who else will be affected if you achieve it?
Who do you know that has already succeeded in achieving this goal?
What external constraints are there to you achieving your goal?
How might you constrain yourself (e.g., motivation, negative thinking etc)?
How might you overcome these obstacles?
What is *really* stopping you?
What might you be doing to sabotage your own efforts to reach this goal?

Options

What could you do as the next step towards reaching your goal?
What else could you do? And what else then?
If time / money / resources / people were not a factor, what could you do?
What would happen if you did nothing?
Who do you admire who already does this well?
What could you do that they do?

Will

Which options appeal most?
How do those options help you in achieving your goal?
Who else needs to know about your goal?
How and when will you inform them?
What obstacles do you expect to meet?
How will you overcome those obstacles?
What other priorities do you have that might divert your energy and motivation?
What will you do first?
How committed are you to moving forward with this, on a scale of 1 (low) - 10 (high)?
What would need to happen for your score to be higher?

My Goal - My Answers

Pick out a selection of questions on the previous page under each of the G-R-O-W headings, and use them to progress your own thinking and ideas about the goal you identified earlier. Write down your answers, here.

Did you manage to progress your thinking?

What could try next time to make it even more effective?

Now try polishing your coaching skills by practising on a friend or colleague.

Coaching to Improve Performance

Understanding personal interference and motivation is key to helping your people get out of their own way. Sometimes, despite best intentions, we manage to trip ourselves up on our journey to peak performance. That's precisely when some good coaching questions really come into their own.

If someone is falling short of their agreed performance, it can be helpful to consider the KASH model to diagnose where the root of the problem might be:

Knowledge:

- What is it that you are trying to achieve here?
- What is the positive difference it will make?
- Do you know how to achieve it?
- Who else do you know who has already achieved this?
- Could you ask them how they did it?

Attitude:

- How do you feel about trying to achieve this?
- Do you believe you can achieve it?
- What are the consequences if you don't manage to do it?

Skills:

- Do you believe that you have the skills to do the task?
- What have you tried already, that has worked?
- What else do you need to learn to help you with this job right now?

Habit:

- Have you tried doing this in the past?
- How many times have you completed it successfully?
- If previous attempts haven't been successful, what else did you try?
- Practice makes perfect. How many times do you need to do this successfully before you know you've cracked it?

Directive (PUSH) Coaching

Author Jack Canfield said "We complain about things that we could change, but have chosen not to, so we complain to vent our frustration at our own inertia."

Just occasionally, some people may get stuck in their thinking about how to tackle a certain issue or complete a specific task, or convince themselves that they'll never be able to resolve it. As a result, you may find yourself coaching them repeatedly on an issue you have already discussed.

STOP IT!

Not only is this a poor use of your time, but it is allowing them to avoid getting started. It may be that they are afraid of failing, or perhaps haven't understood exactly what is required. But sometimes, an individual may secretly be hoping that if they complain enough about it, you will take the problem away and deal with it yourself. The problem gets solved this time, but they don't learn, and you have just added another task to your own to-do list.

Here's what to do instead:

First, summarise your understanding of their issue:

"Ah yes, we've discussed this before, haven't we? Now, as I recall, the key elements are X, Y and Z."

Then, remind them of what they had agreed to do:

"And if I remember rightly, you said you would do A, then B, and finally, C. Have you started on A yet?"

Watch quietly as they shuffle uncomfortably, mumbling excuses, then...

"Right, so go and get started on A right away, please, and let me know how you get on."

Then go back to whatever you were doing, to signify that the conversation is closed, and the onus is now back firmly on them to start taking action.
But remember, the ideas, actions and strategies must be theirs, NOT YOURS, or it creates dependency on you, and they don't own it.

Ensure Success through High Commitment

You know you're doing a great job coaching when you help your people to identify their own solutions with a high level of commitment.

You have been discussing the goals and targets for each person in your team, and using coaching to get them to explore how they could achieve them. Once you have come up with an action plan, you need to test how committed they are to achieving it. One way of checking, is to ask the person to rate their commitment:

"So, on a scale of 1 - 10 (where 10 is 100% committed to achieving this), how committed are you?"

An answer of 1 - 4: oh dear! Time to go back to the start, and make sure they understanding why you are asking them to focus on this particular goal.

- "That seems very low. Tell me what's on your mind?"
- "Oh dear, seems as though you anticipate problems. Let's discuss those now."
- "That's a low score. Tell me about your other priorities."

An answer to 5 - 7: not bad, but still leaves a lot of wriggle-room. Ask more coaching questions to find out what would help their score to be higher:

- "How could we get that score higher, do you think? "
- "What would need to happen for that score to 10 out of 10, instead of only 6?"
- "What could get in the way of your success? And what do you want to do about that? How do you want to overcome that obstacle?"

An answer of 8 - 10: great! But is there still room for improvement with an 8 or a 9?

- "Excellent news! Is there anything else you need from me in order for that to be 10/10?"
- "What will be your first step?"
- If 10/10: "Great! Let's catch up next month to see how you are getting on."

Tip:

When working on a behaviour or performance that needs improvement, be sure to ask the team member to confirm IN WRITING what you have agreed they should work on. That helps to demonstrate that they have really understood. Also, when it's written by them, in their language, and emailed to you from their email account, it will be MUCH harder for them to claim they didn't know what they were supposed to be doing.

Coaching Practice

The best way to test this process and to commit it to memory is to put some of the ideas into practice. You can use this activity to help you prepare for a Crucible Conversation. Work with a friend or colleague to coach you on how to achieve it.

Take it in turn to play each of the following roles:

1. The coaching leader
2. The employee being coached

Use the forms on the following pages to note down your thoughts, ideas, feelings and feedback.

Take as long as you need... don't rush it.

Make a note so that you don't forget:

Round #1:

Coaching leader name:
Employee being coached name:

Round #2:

Coaching leader name:
Employee being coached name:

Round #3:

Coaching leader name:
Employee being coached name:

Coaching Practice: COACHING LEADER

How did I prepare for this discussion?

What frame of mind was I in as we started?

Did my feelings change over the course of our discussion?

Did I help the other person to come to their own solution?

Did I manage to stay out of 'solutions' mode?

Did I test for commitment to the goal / course of action?

Which part of this activity am I most pleased about?

Which element would I definitely do differently next time?

How will I remember to integrate the feedback I received here into my coaching practice?

Reward and Recognition

The best way to encourage good performance is to reward it every time it happens, until it becomes a habit.

This simple formula will help you to improve the performance and behavior of every one of your team members.

Catch them doing something right. When someone has a great idea, supports a colleague, goes the extra mile by making an extra effort, be sure to say thank you.

Some leaders take the view that if you say thank you, you risk encouraging complacency. But try not saying thank you, and run the risk of your employees believing that you take them for granted. The results will be much worse.

Occasionally, a leader will say that they don't need to say thank you. The very fact that their employee still has a job should surely be thanks enough. However, high performing staff will be more likely to look for a job elsewhere if they think you haven't noticed their efforts. "You don't know how lucky you are" rarely convinces a motivated employee.

Many people think of 'reward' as being financial, and worry that they don't have the budget available to give a discretionary bonus or grant a pay rise. In truth, however, reward can take many forms. Chocolate, going home on time, training courses, flexible working hours... all of these can be used to reward good performance.

How many other types of reward can you identify?

A person who feels appreciated will always do more than expected.

Alternatives to Financial Reward

You may not have a big budget or be able to afford to pay your team members the amount they think they deserve. But you can consider other elements of motivation - such as personal and professional aspirations - and think about meeting some of those needs, instead. How can you give them more of what they really want? The SPACE analysis will provide some important clues.

For example, paying for a recognised qualification (HNC, NVQs, PRINCE2 or other professional qualification) will make them a more desirable employee, and give them greater employment security.

But what happens if you train your people, and then they leave, I hear you ask. Ah, but what if you don't train them, and they stay?

What other non-financial rewards could you provide to your team?

Leading Organizational Change

Much of the role of leadership will be setting the tone and pace for change. The concept of change often strikes fear into the hearts and minds of managers and employees alike, but it is an unavoidable part of organizational survival.

Since the word 'change' carries so many negative connotations, perhaps you might consider using the language of 'evolution' instead. Evolution is about survival in response to external factors, and it can be helpful to point out to your people all the big evolutionary steps the business has already taken to bring you to this point.

Crucially, by constantly surveying the marketplace and being aware of industry trends, we can lead business change before it is forced upon us.

The Critical Angle of Delay: Don't Leave it Too Late

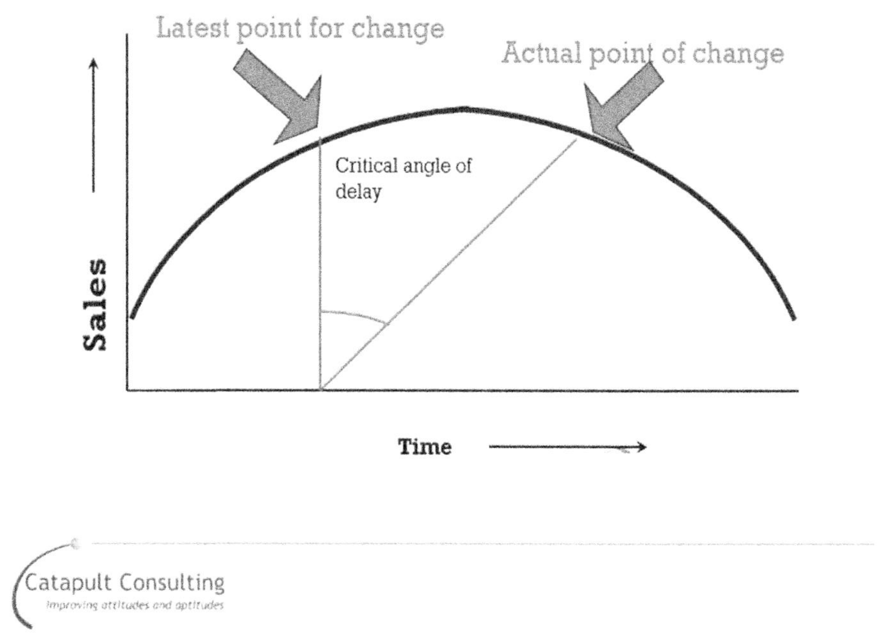

Fear of the unknown often means that leaders are slow to embrace the need for organizational change.

There will be many external and internal factors driving the need to change. Are you awake and aware of those drivers? Do you discuss them regularly during leadership team meetings to check if you need to take urgent action?

The Story of Five Frogs on a Log
(a story about change hesitation)

Once upon a time, there were five frogs, sat on a log in the middle of a gently meandering stream. Day by pleasant day, they sat on their log, catching flies, jumping in for a refreshing dip, and then chatting amongst themselves about Log-Life.

As the days rolled by, then began to notice a curious phenomenon; when they jumped into the river, they found they were having to swim harder and faster to get back onto the log. The river, it seemed, was no longer meandering, but flowing quite freely now. Even when they were sat on the log, they couldn't help noticing that the river bank was running past them a good bit faster than it had. The tallest frog stood on his hind legs and looked behind him at the section of river they had already passed. Then he looked ahead, and noticed that the river seemed to be flowing even faster ahead, and that it was much noisier. The frogs realised that the log was gaining pace because it was heading towards a waterfall. They talked about what might happen if they went over the waterfall. What was on the other side? They couldn't think of any other frogs who had ever been over a waterfall before who could have told them what it was like. Maybe it would be cool, refreshing, crystal clear water, with lots of tasty bugs just lounging around, waiting to be eaten. But maybe it was full of herons with a penchant for frogs' legs, ready to eat them. The story of the herons filled them with so much fear and dread, that they decided that the best course of action was to stay on the banks of the river they knew so well, and carry on their happy life there. So, they decided to get off the log. They talked about getting off the log. They talked about how they would get off in the faster flowing river, and where they would swim to. They talked about when they would get off, and who would get off first. They decided they would all get off together. They decided they would get off in the morning, but for now, they would sleep. Next day never came; they were washed over the waterfall, and smashed to smithereens on the rocks at the bottom. And so it was; all five frogs knew they needed to change, all five agreed to do it, but they waited too long to take action, and the herons had a feast the following morning.

The moral of the story is simple: scan your horizon, make a plan, and TAKE ACTION! The commercial graveyards of history are full of log-frogs: Oddbins, Blockbuster, Encyclopaedia Britannica, Kodak, Tie Rack, Blackberry, Pan Am, Enron, Forbo Lancaster, MySpace.. this depressing list grows year by year. These are organizations who lost out - and some disappeared completely - because they were complacent, or simply didn't respond quickly enough in a fast-changing market.

Sometimes, the enormity of major organizational transformation feels overwhelming, and anticipating resistance from employees, leaders lack the courage of their convections and opt for a safer and more transactional approach to change. In other words, change emerges, little by little, reactively, in response to supply chain pressure, shifting market conditions, competitor activity and the ease (or otherwise) of attracting, recruiting and retaining the best talent. And then there's liquidity, of course. Cash flow is a real issue to consider when planning change. The bigger the change, the more money we often need to invest, and often the longer we have to wait before we see a return on the investment. You might argue that that is good corporate practice, not to spend large amounts of money and end up highly leveraged. But step by step short-termism might keep the bank balance steady now, but may lead to a shorter life expectancy.

Many organizations hesitate to effect major change programs because they are complacent about the need to change, or fear getting it wrong, or don't take big enough action.

The absolute worst reason for avoiding change is that the executive team are approaching retirement and don't want the hassle. DON'T let your inaction be the reason your organization fails.

Over the page, write a list of all the reasons you need to make change happen. On the facing page, list all of the reasons you can imagine to avoid making transformational change.

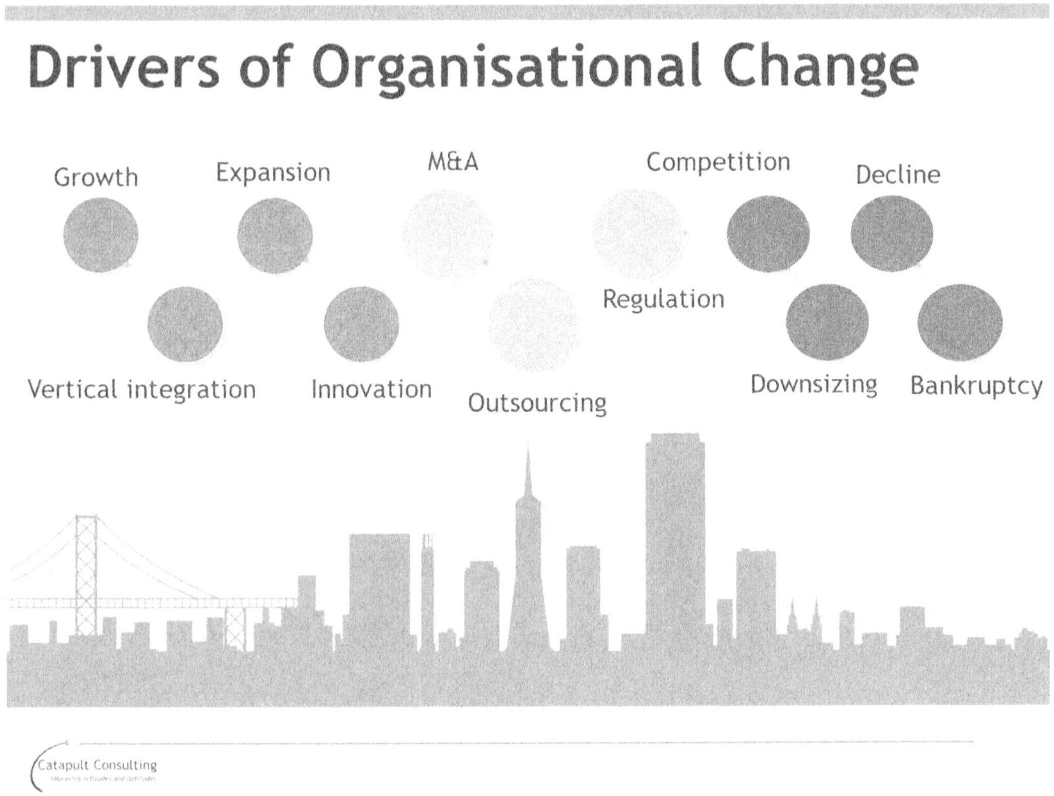

Drivers of major transformation of our enterprise:

- What are the reasons driving your need for business change?

Reasons for avoiding change:

- What reasons are you hearing / can you think of for not embracing change?

Understanding the Roots of Resistance to Change

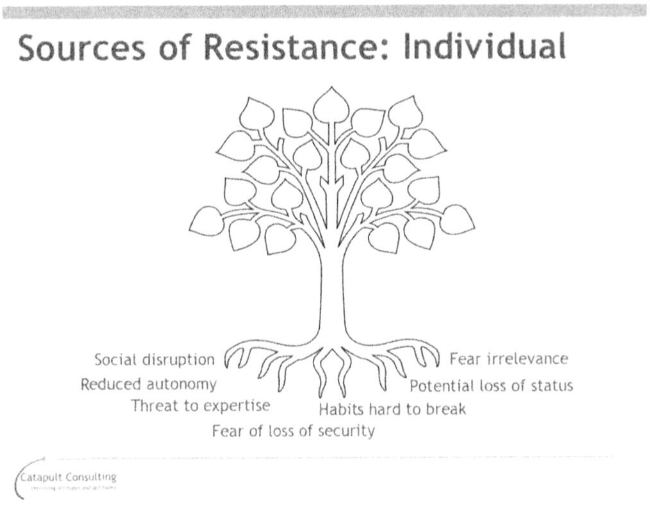

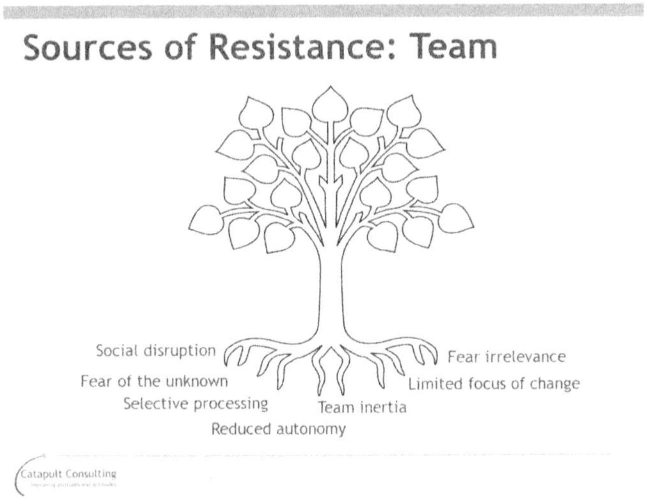

Resistance Can Be Helpful

- All consequences may not have been thought through
- Resistance ensures organisation can hold on to things it values including this change
- Avoids being derailed by new fads
- Conflict shown to strengthen subsequent commitment
- Also improves the quality of decision-making
- A source of good feedback on the change.
- Keeps the organisation 'honest'
- '*Retrotopia*': what was good about the old way that we want to preserve into the new?
- Pre-mortem as a healthy way to surface resistance

Catapult Consulting

How does resistance to change serve your organization?

Response to Change

The change curve below is based on the grief curve as defined by Elizabeth Kubler-Ross. In this version, we identify the natural human response to the upheaval brought about by organizational change. It is helpful to understand the emotional response, because until employees have processed the first three stages, they will be unable to embrace the proposed change, no matter how logical you think it is.

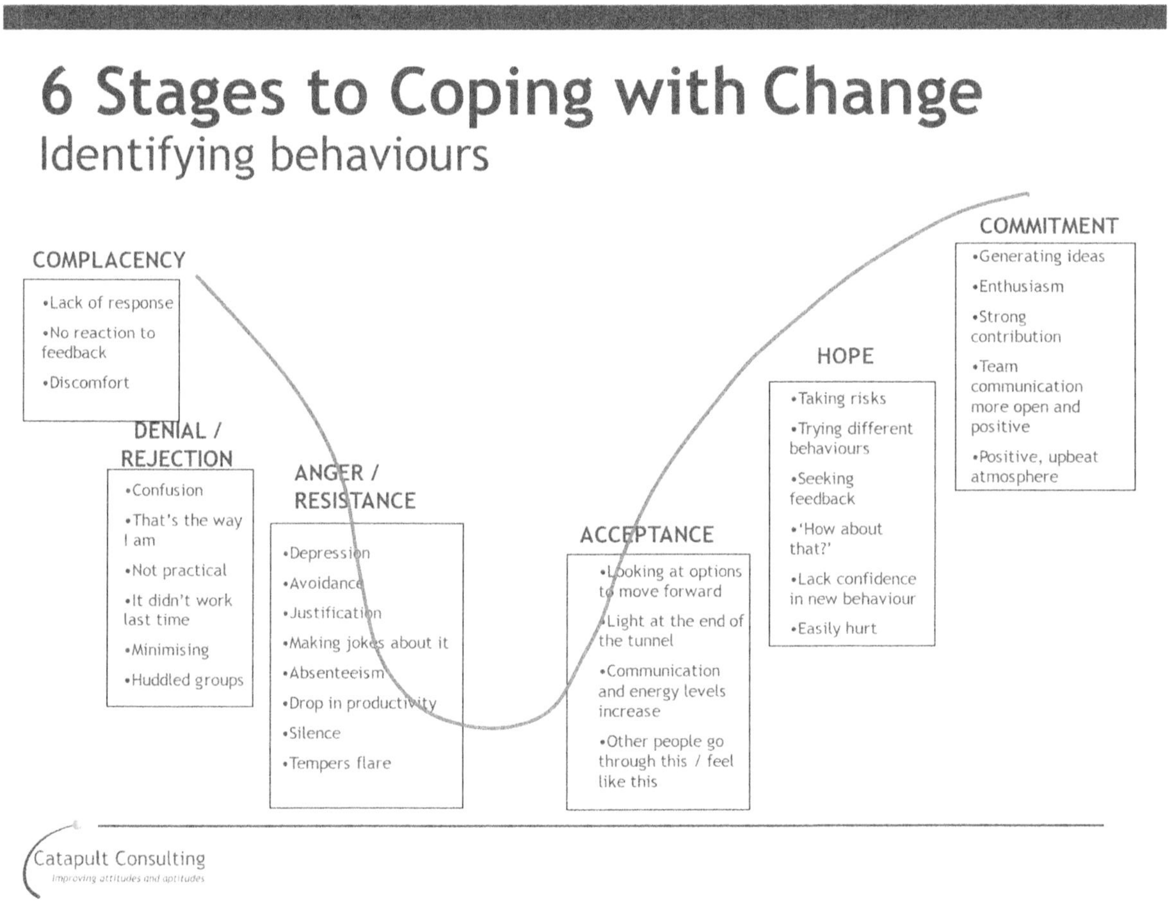

Employee behaviour will tend to follow this pattern. The model above is helpful to guide you in identifying whereabouts they are on the change curve.

The model below prompts you on how to communicate to employees affected by change, at each stage of the response.

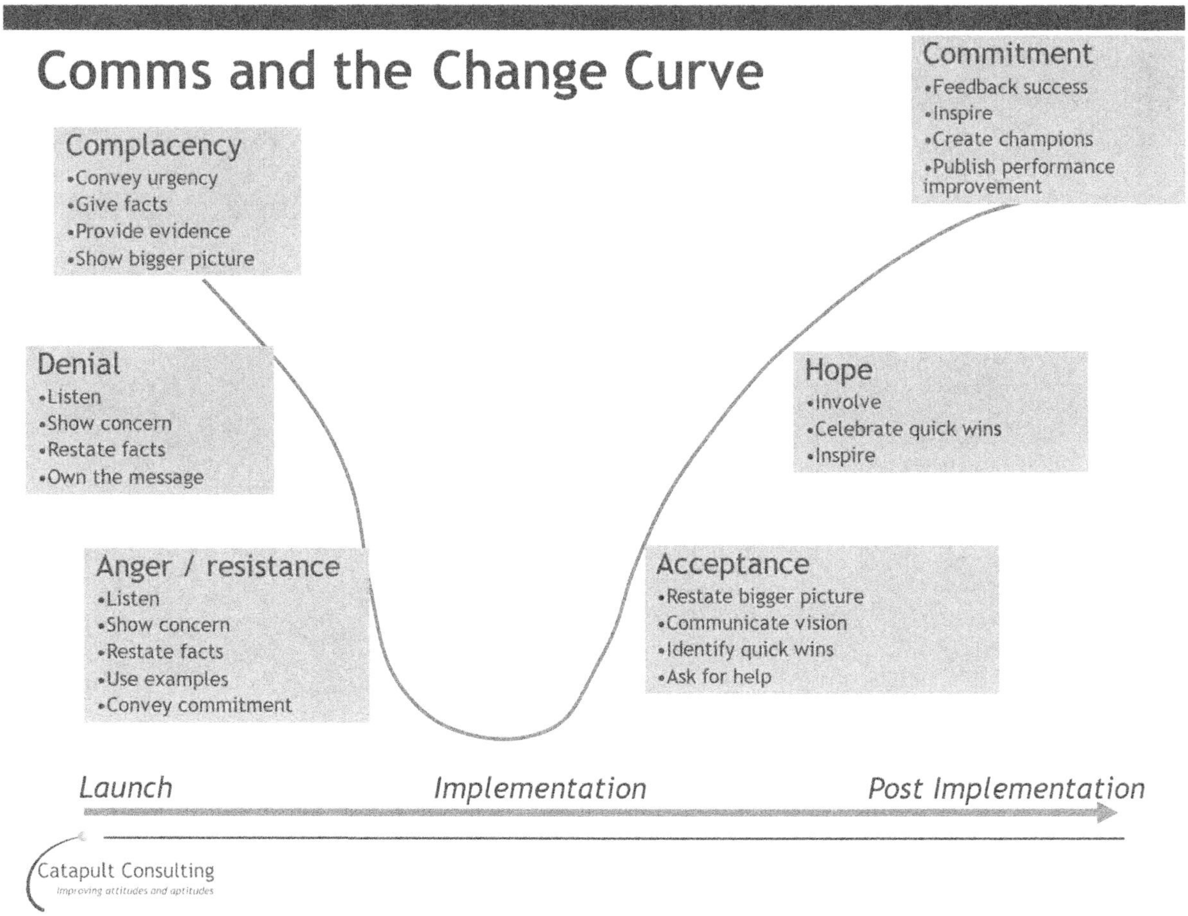

Change Overload

Your people will likely become more exhausted by change when there are several changes happening simultaneously in their personal and professional lives.

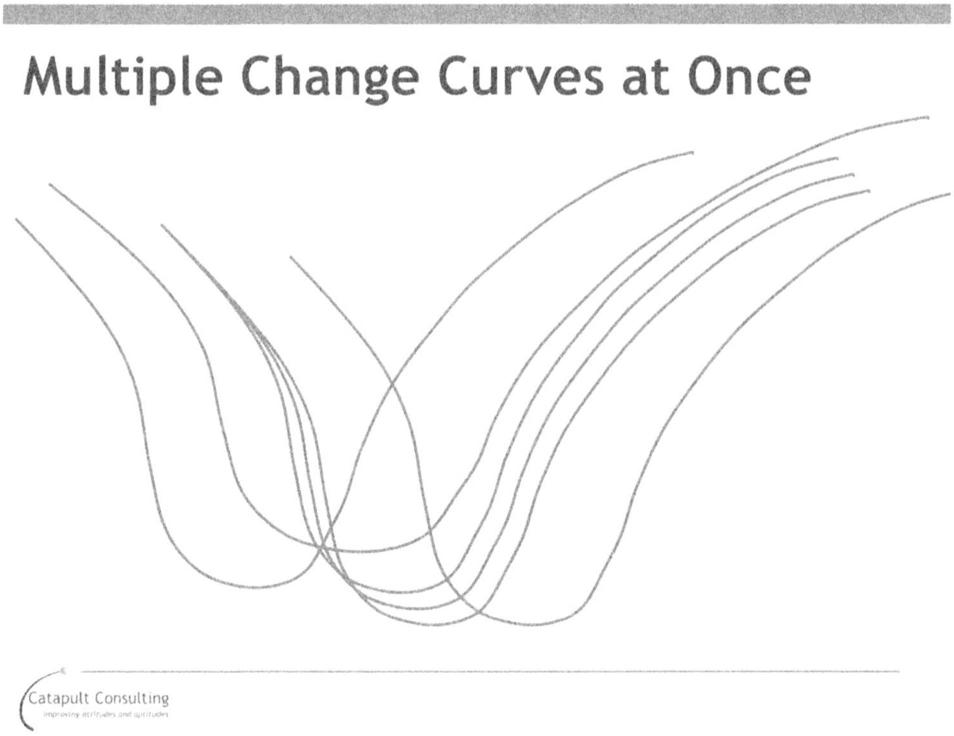

And let's not forget that that the change curve doesn't just go from left to right. Your employees might be working through their response, and then experience a setback, which takes them back a step or two.

Change that is well communicated and well managed will mean that people spend less time in the change curve, often feeling more engaged at the end of the change than at the beginning.

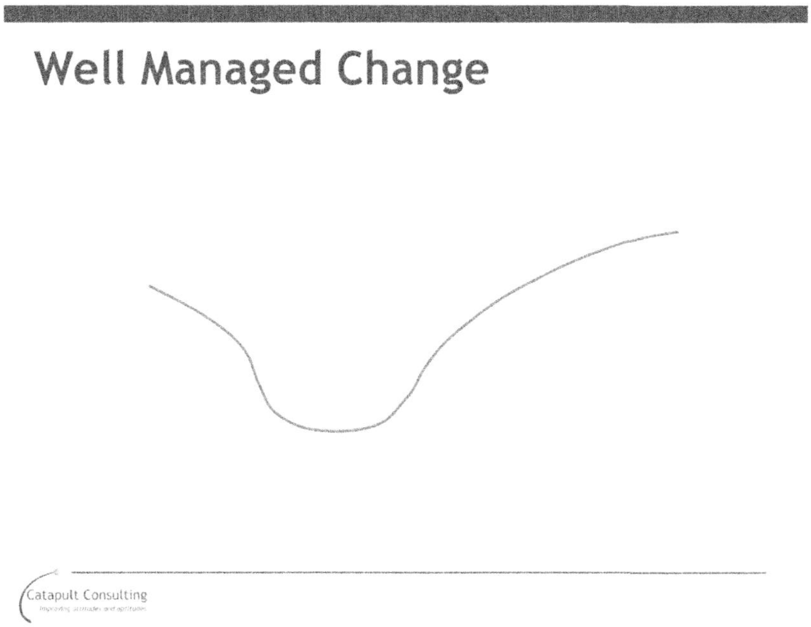

Change that is chaotic, however, and badly managed, can eave employees languishing for an extended period, where engagement, productivity, customer satisfaction, and ultimately, PROFIT will all suffer.

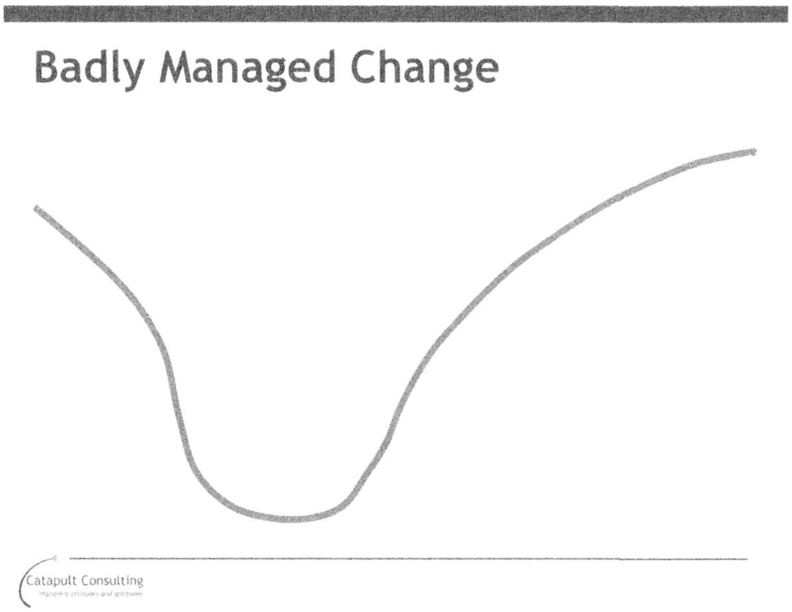

Double Helix Change Curve

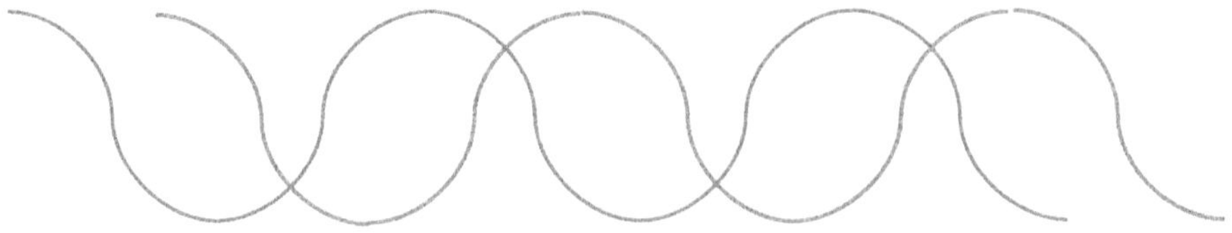

Leaders' response to change
Employees' response to change

Catapult Consulting
Improving attitudes and aptitudes

The double helix represents the change curve which you experience as you lead the change. You will normally have a head start on your employees, and just as you are coming to terms with how change will impact on you, you are trying to be positive in your communication to others. It can be a particularly tough time for leaders!

Throughout the change and uncertainty, everyone will be looking to you for the answers - answers which you may not yet have.

The key here is to keep the dialogue open. Give people a part to play in change which affects them. Not only is it a powerful way to manage change resistance, they will often be best placed to understand the operational reality of what you are trying to achieve.

Tip: Listen to your people!

I have interviewed many leaders from around the globe about their biggest lesson as a leader, and the answer is surprisingly consistent. Listen to your people, and don't assume you have all the answers.

Ask The Right Questions

- Is your leadership team fully aligned with the changes you are planning?
- Are you absolutely 100% certain about that?
- Is it safe to discuss areas of disagreement, or does everyone just comply?
- Do they know why the organization exists?
- Are they clear on how they can deliver your strategic imperatives?
- Do you have real strategic alignment across the business?
- And do all of your employees understand how their work contributes to the bigger picture?

These are just a few of the vital questions that don't get asked in business because people are all too busy doing the business to check if everyone agrees on what 'the business' actually is. It is critical to ask the right questions for testing clarity, understanding and buy-in which can help to identify areas of concern in a safe and respectful way. A carefully facilitated conversation with the leadership and management teams can be a powerful way to elicit any and every area of confusion, dissent, cannibalisation and sabotage. At the end of this this activity, you will hopefully have a leadership team which is 100% aligned with the business goal. In fact, you cannot realistically hope to achieve a high-performance culture without asking these questions which are so crucial to your success.

Starting with Simon Sinek "Why, not what", when you are clear about the why, your big-brained employees will usually have lots of great ideas to support the what, and the how. In turn, this will support your performance management process, your likely success at managing and implementing wider organizational change, the quality and quantitative of communication, and the effectiveness of your leadership.

Case Study - Fit for the Future

In September 2017, Catapult Consulting was asked by a public sector client to investigate why their ambitious change programme had failed to deliver on any of its objectives.

Communication is always key to successful change implementation, so we started there. The programme had been launched nearly three years earlier, but leadership communication had dried up over a year before. "There's a big clue!" we suggested, but the HR Director looked awkward. "That mustn't be the answer. Please - there must be something else."

Why wasn't the lack of comms allowed to be the answer? Who was managing the change comms strategy? And why did nobody want to discuss change comms with us? We dug deeper, running a series of focus groups with staff selected from various parts of the organization, including the employee forum, business improvement team, and the comms team. There was confusion about the programme; most people were surprised to hear it being mentioned. "I thought that had died a long time ago!" was a common response. We dug deeper still, holding a series of 1:1 meetings with the senior managers and other go-to people. Their understanding was vague and contradictory. We interviewed each member of the executive team. The CEO was very clear about the reason for the change programme. Fit for the Future was his idea. But we quickly discovered that the CEO was the only member of the exec team who thought it was a good idea. All the rest of the directors thought the programme was ill-conceived, impractical and unrealistic. "Have you raised this with the CEO?" we asked. "No, he doesn't want to hear it", came the overwhelming reply.

We wrote up a list of anonymised findings to protect the confidences shared, with recommendations for a relaunch and comms plan. But our recommendations included some very specific activities designed to check alignment and surface concerns. We met again with the CEO, and discussed our findings, including resistance from within his team. The mood became ugly very quickly. "They are all fully on board!" he insisted. "They are not, and we'll prove it to you" we replied. We carried out a group activity with the wider exec team, surfacing issues and discussing anticipated problems, then followed with a powerful intervention designed to promote alignment and ownership. The programme was relaunched company-wide, and has finally proven to be a great success, achieving all of its 9 strategic imperatives.

We should never take for granted that the most senior and experienced leaders of an organization are all in agreement on every aspect of strategic planning. It is fundamental to ensuring that everyone is pulling in the same direction, and communication gets done right the first time.

Kotter's Eight Steps for Leading Change

The author lectures on the subject of Leading Change at master's degree level at several well-respected universities, and Kotter is a popular proponent of change leadership. He proposed a simple 8-Step approach, and this model is our toolkit, used every time we work with client organizations to facilitate change.

Kotter's 8 Steps

1. Create a sense of urgency
2. Build and maintain a guiding coalition
3. Create a vision to direct the change effort
4. Communicate the vision
5. Empower others to act on the vision
6. Plan for and create short-term wins
7. Consolidate improvements, producing further change
8. Institutionalise strategic changes in the culture

Catapult Consulting

Which of these steps were missing in the case study on the previous page?

Leadership Communication

80% of a leader's job is communication, and regardless of how many channels of communication exist within your organization, your team will look to you to keep them informed about matters which affect them, and keep them focused on the right things in order to deliver the vision, mission and strategy.

During periods of change and uncertainty - well, that's pretty much ALL of the time! - your people will look to their leadership team for guidance and reassurance.

Sometimes, you may not have all the answers, but by having a clear vision, and helping all employees to see how they can contribute to organizational success, your staff will feel more secure because they know what is expected of them.

As explored earlier, the primary role of leadership is to create a compelling vision for the future, and then to remind employees regularly about that vision, so that people remain focused on the right things.

One way to focus people is through the daily interactions you have with them, at the water cooler, in the elevator, or walking in from the car park together. This is called microleadership, and it sits at the heart of strategic alignment, coaching, excellent communication skills and a high-performance culture.

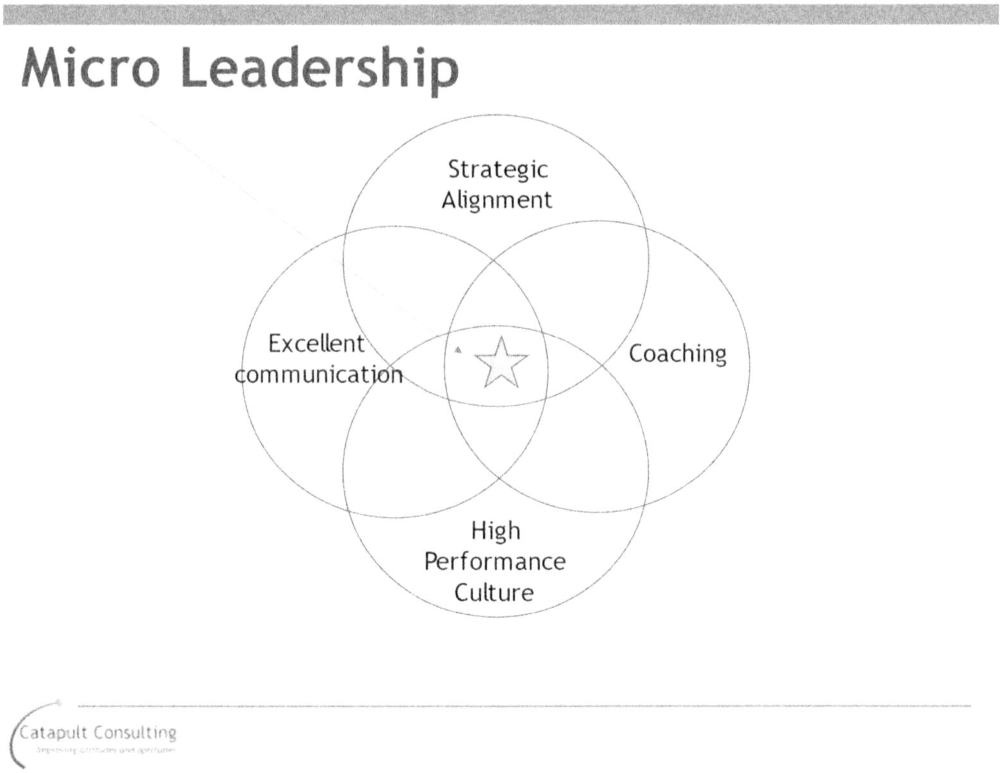

Micro Leadership: 21st Century Orgs

What it is:

- A tool to help your people see how their contribution matters
- A way to get employees focusing on the things of strategic importance
- A method for encouraging innovation of products and services
- A powerful route to effective prioritisation
- A high impact trust builder
- A great way to build relationships
- Incredibly empowering
- A key driver of employee engagement

What it is NOT:

- Micro-management by another name
- Something that only a leader can do
- Political game playing

Catapult Consulting
Improving attitudes and aptitudes

Micro Leadership Questions

That article about our biggest competitor… What might that mean for us?
Did you read that piece about innovation within our industry? How could we use that?
What are the innovations in our supplier sectors that we could capitalise upon?
Tell me what part you play in helping to deliver our vision?
Can you name me one of our strategic imperatives for this year?
What knowledge, skills and experience do you have that we could be putting to better use?
What could the recent changes in legislation mean for us?
What steps should we take to create a higher performance culture here?
How has your work contributed to our business goals this week?
Do you feel like your (our) work makes a difference to the world?
How can we help our customers to feel better served by us?
What should we be doing today to make our competitors irrelevant?

Catapult Consulting
Improving attitudes and aptitudes

What other micro leadership questions could you ask your people?

Help People to Understand WHY

Rocket launcher.

You may see a brush. But in 1968 Joe Saltzer, a cleaner working for NASA saw it differently. When asked by a visitor what he did, he replied, *"I'm helping to put a man on the moon."*

Catapult Consulting

The story may be apocryphal, but the message is the same. Help each person in your team to understand exactly how their role contributes towards the success of the organization. It's a key driver of engagement.

What is the message you will share with your people to help them make the connection?

Contextualising

Putting the message in the context of the business priorities ensures that the impact is understood more effectively.

Catapult Consulting

Keep making the connection...

Localising

Adapting global messages, ideas and content to the needs of your audience will capture attention and ensure improved understanding.

Catapult Consulting

Activity: Contextualising and Localising

One group to 'personalise' a section of a recent announcement, adding local stories and statistics, removing any jargon, so that the message resonates at a local level.

One group to identify a local objective which their team is working on, ask a series of 'why are we doing this?' questions, and demonstrate how this work contributes to the overall strategy.

Share your thinking.

Catapult Consulting
Improving attitudes and aptitudes

Feedback

Communication is not a one-way street

Need to test audience

- Ask them to paraphrase
- Ask someone to summarise
- Ask someone to re-read
- Ask questions to test understanding
- Ask for audience opinions on the message

- They haven't necessarily heard what you said
- You may need to repeat the message several times
- Invite questions and allow all discussion
- Park what you can't answer
- Understanding reactions is critical!

Catapult Consulting

You ask for questions and feedback, but nobody says a word!

1. They didn't understand
2. They are shocked
3. They are afraid of what the message may mean for them
4. They are still digesting the message
5. They don't know what questions to ask… yet
6. They don't want to look foolish in front of their colleagues
7. The Unions have told them not to respond
8. They don't want to appear to be a troublemaker
9. They don't trust the speaker, and would prefer to discuss with their line manager
10. They are too shy to speak up in front of a crowd
11. They are worried about recrimination as a result of speaking up
12. They are too embarrassed to admit that they weren't listening.

Tip: take it offline!

Invite people to email questions, ask their employee rep, or give out Post-It notes for anonymous feedback. And observe the body language shown by your audience.

How will you check for feedback following future announcements?

The channel of communication your people rely on most is... YOU!

During periods of change and uncertainty, employees often complain that nobody ever tells them what is going on. There is probably a lot of information being transmitted to staff, but people have a tendency to ignore unpopular or difficult messages and instead complain that their managers keep them in the dark.

List below all the messages you need to share with your people.

-
-
-
-
-
-
-
-
-
-

Then for each of the messages, rate the degree of change (1 = low, 5 = high).

Next, rate how much your people need to play an active role in making the change happen (1 = low, 5 = high).

Now, consider the balance between the degree of change that is happening, and the degree of engagement you need from your audience. The communications escalator, below, will help you to select the most appropriate channel to convey your message.

If the change is a small change - for example "From next month, expenses claim form ABC1 is being replaced by DEF2, which can be found in the usual place on the intranet", you just need to notify people by email, signpost on the intranet, newsletter or a message on the staff notice board.

But if the announcement is about major change, for example "From January 1st next year, this office will be closing permanently, and instead we will be transitioning to full-time remote working." This announcement will have a much bigger impact on your people, and they will likely have lots of questions about the proposed change. If you need them to be fully committed with the change, you should use a combination of conferences, team exercises, team objectives, and regular in-person updates.

Comms Escalator

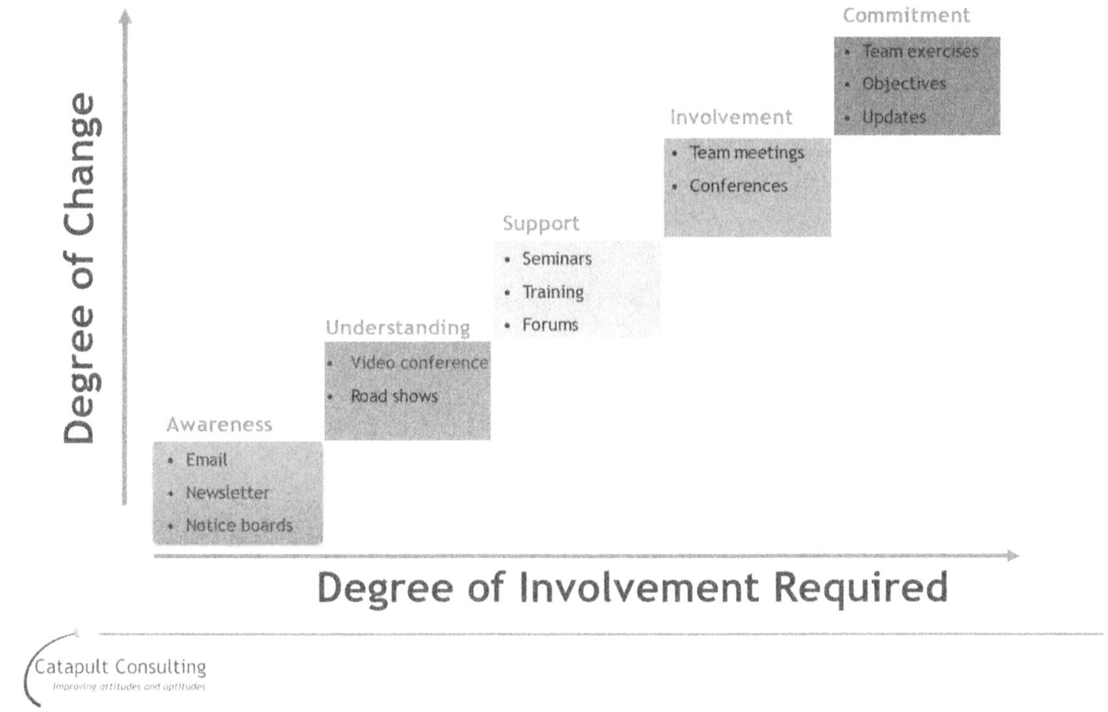

How can you use the comms escalator to plan for higher impact communication which engages both hearts and minds?

Now let's consider the tone of your message.

Degrees of Involvement

- Telling : 'We have to do this'
- Selling: ' We have the answer - Lets see if we can get your buy - in'
- Testing: 'What works - What doesn't'
- Consulting: 'What vision should we adopt'
- Co - Creating : Lets create the vision we individually and collectively want

Catapult Consulting

What has been your preferred style, previously?

Which style might serve you better?

Towards / away from:

Give people a positive and emotionally compelling reason the change, and they are more likely to engage. Give them a change-or-die reason, and they are more likely to freeze, and then hope it goes away.

Golden Rules of Communication

1. One version of the truth
2. You cannot NOT communicate
3. Say as much as you can, as soon as you can
4. Own the message
5. Check for feedback
6. The response you get = the message you gave
7. Walk your own talk
8. Match the message and medium
9. Flex your style to suit all audiences
10. The bigger the message, the more face to face
11. 'Spin' damages trust permanently
12. Communication = 80% of a leader's job

Catapult Consulting

Which best describes your business communication: high calorie, low nutritional value (lots of waffly messages), or high in nutrition, low in calories (succinct messages with new, actionable information)?

Measuring the Effectiveness of Communication

- Number of publications per annum
- Frequency and attendance at team briefings
- Viewing levels of corporate videos

versus

- Understanding
- Attitude
- Behavioural change

Catapult Consulting

It can be difficult meaningfully to measure the impact of your communication effectiveness as a leader. It isn't just about the number of channels you have at your disposal, or the number of messages you send.

Ask yourself this:

Is it resulting in better understanding, great attitude, and improved behaviour?

If not, you're not getting the comms piece quite right. You can always ask your people what they want to know, and remember to use your monthly 1:1 face to face meetings to check in with each employee and provide additional context to the messages they have heard throughout the month.

Stakeholder Management

In our increasingly complex organizations, you will regularly find that you have responsibility without authority, or are working in a highly political organization where people are nervous of being seen to do the wrong thing, or risk upsetting their colleagues. Matrix structure organizations - whilst they may offer high levels of operational agility, often bring complexity when it comes to understanding who is working on what, and who is on whose side.

As we said at the outset, if you don't understand people, you don't understand business. People will work better with people they like, so this section is all about understanding some of the subtleties of organizational politics, and how you can use your power and influence effectively and ethically to get the job done.

Everyone says that they hate office politics; however, politics is all about lobbying for support - for your project, for your team, for your organizational priorities. The difference between good politics and bad politics is as simple as looking at whose interests are being served by a course of action. If a player in an organization is taking credit for the work of others, demanding more staff, pushing for a change in job title, with all the associated personal benefits of salary and other rewards, it is plain to see that their use of power and influence is self-serving. That is the ugly side of corporate game-playing. If a player is completely transparent about their motives, linking each request they make of others to the organizational purpose, vision and strategic goals, when they give credit rather than take it, when they always defend their team in public and challenge them in private, that is good politics, and shows great integrity in the use of influence.

Over the next couple of pages there is some current academic thinking about leadership, power and influence. As you read through this section, be mindful of your own style of influence, and also the styles of those other leaders who are trusted throughout your organization.

A brief word on corporate psychopaths: it is mercifully still fairly rare to find yourself working with a corporate psychopath. Psychopathic behaviour tends to be highly self-serving, and these individuals may be charming and witty to their seniors, whilst driving their direct reports with manipulation, bullying and humiliation. The damage they can do to staff retention - and corporate reputation - should not be underestimated, so you should take any complaints from staff seriously, particularly if there is a common theme to their concerns.

Understanding Power

- **Reward power**
  - Formal or informal, assumes authority to lead, built on rewards, common, effective short term
- **Positional (formal) power**
  - Formal, delegated, authority to lead, reward / coercive power, most common, quite effective
- **Coercive power**
  - Formal / informal, assumes authority to lead, built on coercion (and bullying), still common in some organisations, least effective
- **Relational power**
  - Ask, not tell, the go-to person, invests in relationship, building 'credit', most effective in the long term, best in complex organisational structures
- **Knowledge power**
  - May share or withhold information, short term, but very powerful- whose agenda? Need to manage carefully!

Catapult Consulting
improving attitudes and aptitudes

Which is your power style?

And what is the predominant power style within your organization?

How effective is each style within your organizational context?

McLelland identified that every human being will have one or more of the following cognitive needs. Understanding what drives individual behavior gives us a deeper understanding into what makes people 'tick'.

McLelland's Cognitive Needs

A set of key psychological needs that may be particularly relevant in a work context:

- **Achievement:** Getting things done, successful accomplishment of goals, clarity of purpose, making things happen, *fear failure*
- **Affiliation:** Connecting with others; feeling part of something, feeling liked, *fear loneliness*
- **Autonomy:** Having the freedom to decide what to do and how to do it, controlling what happens to you, *fear dependence on others*
- **Power:** Influencing outcomes; being responsible for controlling events, making things happen right, *fear risk-taking*
- **Order:** Controlling ambiguity; creating certainty and predictability, clarity of understanding; *fear mental overload*
- **Status:** Gaining and maintaining the respect and positive regard of others, feeling valued, significant; *fear worthlessness*

Catapult Consulting

Which is your primary cognitive need?

Understanding the above can help us to make sense of how others behave and how their priorities may be different from ours. It also helps to diagnose what people fear, and by association, what they will work hardest to protect.

Managing Diverse Stakeholders

- Who are your key stakeholders?
  - Map them!
  - Who is of primary (P) and who is of secondary (S) importance to helping you get the job done?
  - Thickness of the line between you and them denotes the weight of comms traffic between you
  - Which is your go-to channel of communication with them?
  - Is it the most appropriate?
- How do you usually respond to them?
- How could you choose to respond differently?
- How would that help you?
- Would you feel more empowered?
- Would you be more accountable as a result?

Catapult Consulting

Stakeholders are different to shareholders. Shareholders will usually benefit financially from the success of your business, based on their own financial investment in the company. Stakeholders are people with the ability to influence your business. They can be incredibly helpful, well-connected individuals who are committed to helping the business grow. Or they might be regulators who want to ensure that the business works ethically and legally.

Some of your stakeholders will be senior to you, or your peers, perhaps. Others may be junior to you, but are still key to the success of your organization. Some stakeholders may be clients, or key suppliers. Perhaps you need to include the regulator as a stakeholder, and any other external agency which has the ability to help or hinder business success.

Make a list of all your key stakeholders, here:

For each stakeholder, take a moment to decide if they are a primary stakeholder - you can't really do your job without having them on side - or a secondary stakeholder, in other words, you could probably work around them if you had to.

Stakeholder name	Primary stakeholder (P)?	Secondary stakeholder (S)?

Over the page, you will see that there is a skeleton stakeholder map for you to complete. Your name is at the centre of the map. For each radial, please add the name of a specific stakeholder. Try to use the individual's name so that you can personalise your approach to working with them.

For each name, please add P (for primary) or S (for secondary), depending on their significance to your role.

Once you have added the names, please add thickness to each line, according to the amount of communication that passes between you and each stakeholder.

Then add an arrow to denote the main direction of communication. Is it you who usually contacts them or the other way around?

Finally, look at which channel of communication you rely on to keep your stakeholder informed and engaged.

Ask yourself: is the flow of communication sufficient, given the significance of each stakeholder? Are you spending too much time communicating with some and not enough time with others? Are you waiting for them to contact you, or would it be better for you to initiate more of the communication?

And is the choice of channel of communication appropriate for the job? Could you improve the flow of communication if you spent more time talking face to face?

Worked example:

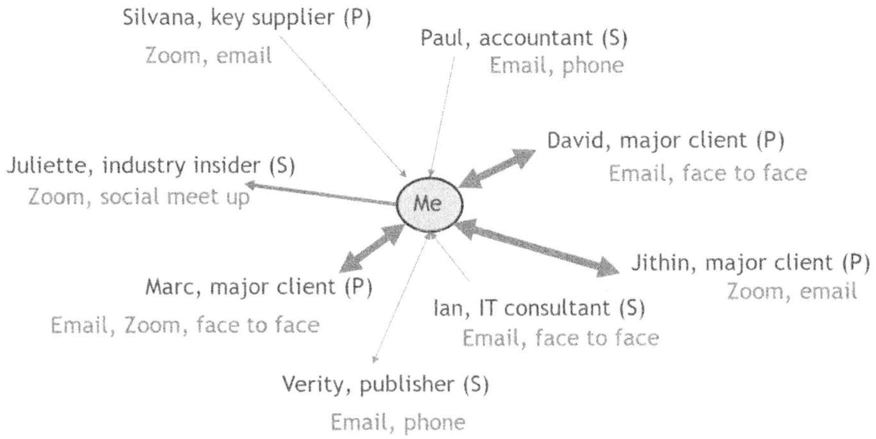

Your Stakeholder Map

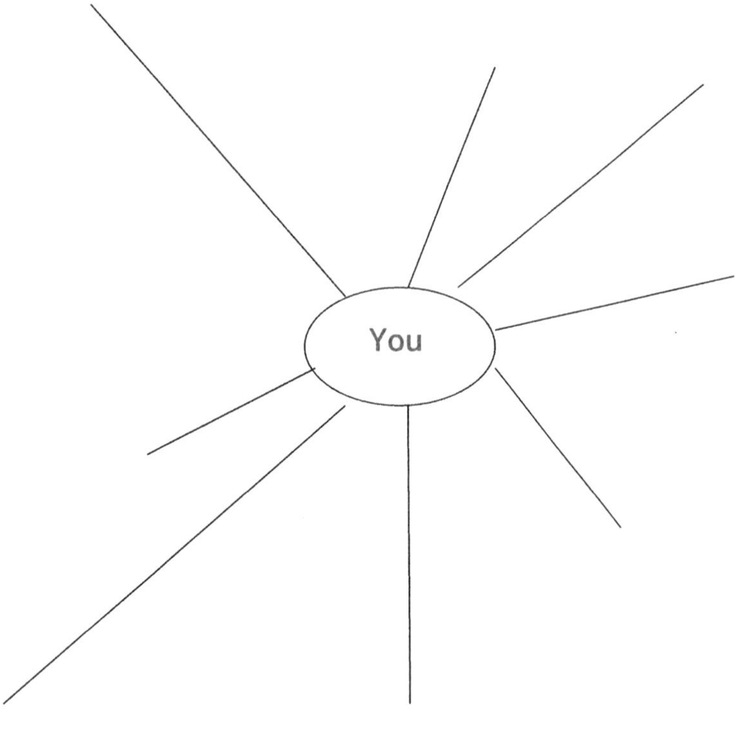

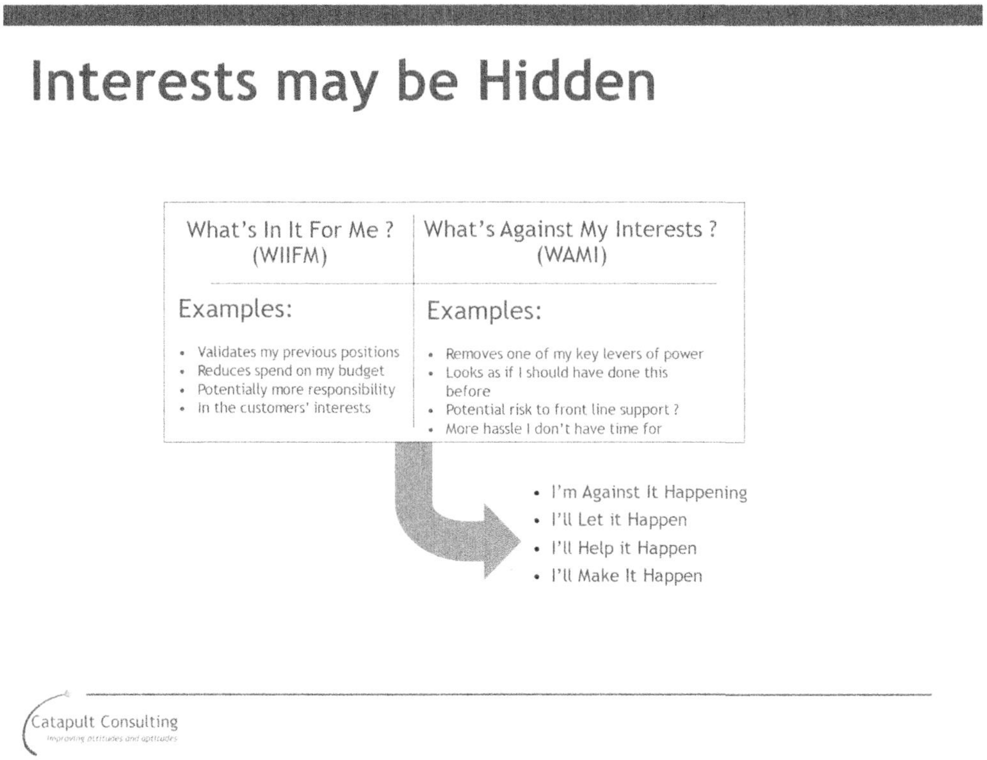

When considering each of your stakeholders, or when preparing an important announcement, it is helpful to spend a moment reflecting on your message, and how they will receive it.

What's in it for them?

Why should they care about your announcement? Will it make their lives easier? Will they benefit personally? If they can see clearly what's in it for them, they will be more receptive to your message.

What's against their interests?

Does your message mean more work for them, less certainty, more change and upheaval? Will they be negatively impacted by the content of your message? If so, you will need to address their concerns even before they raise them.

Their response will determine the degree of support they will offer.

Stakeholder Positions are Visible

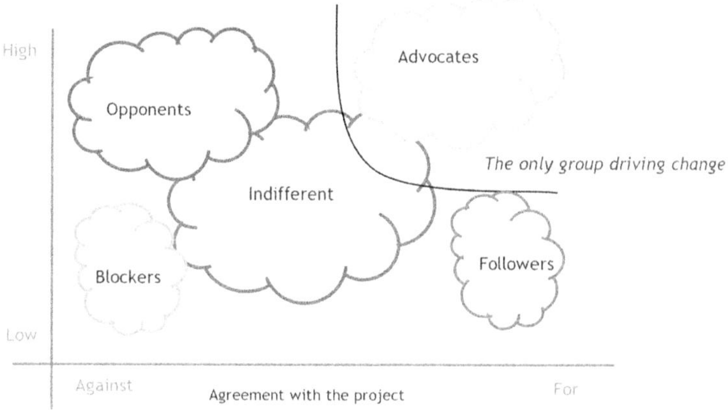

Catapult Consulting

For each stakeholder group, identify:

a) Which behaviours you are likely to see

b) How to manage that stakeholder group

c) What NOT to do.

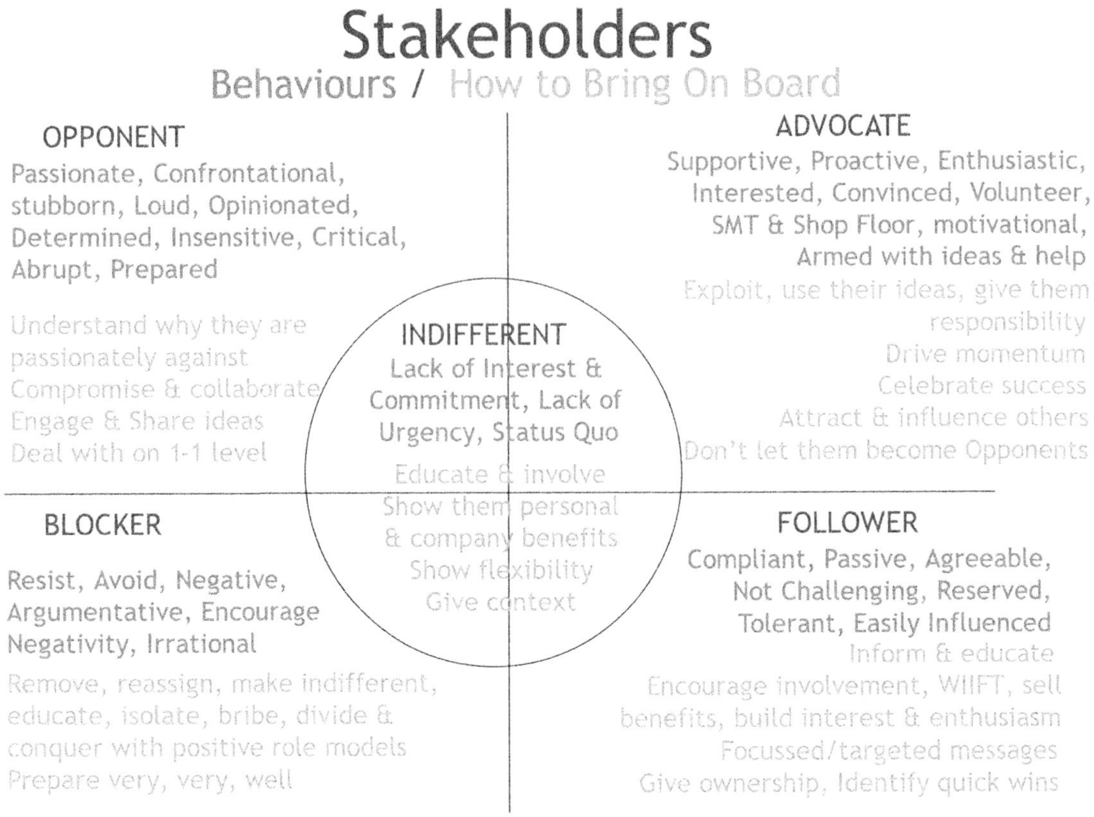

When you can identify their type according to their behaviours, you now also know how to manage them to ensure that they are working to your own clear and transparent agenda, rather than their own agenda.

Psychologist Robert Cialdini explored key themes in the ethical use of influence. His book is referenced in the 'further reading' section.

Cialdini: Science of Persuasion

6 SHORTCUTS
1. RECIPROCITY
2. SCARCITY
3. AUTHORITY
4. CONSISTENCY
5. LIKING
6. CONSENSUS

- Categorise 6 areas into transactional vs transformational
- Which of these are your go-to strategies?
- What could you be using to be more strategically persuasive?
- Which strategy will work best for each of your key stakeholders?
- Specific examples, activities and action plan.

Catapult Consulting

Leadership is influencing others. How could you use each approach, ethically?

Reciprocity (we want to return favours):

Scarcity (we want something more when it is less available to us):

Authority (we are more inclined to comply with people in authority):

Consistency (we like to be consistent with previous opinions and actions):

Liking (we like to cooperate with others who we perceive to be like us):

Consensus (we like to follow the lead of other people, especially those we respect):

Future by Default

The definition of insanity is repeating the same behaviours and expecting a different outcome

Albert Einstein

Change

- Don't let yourself fall back on old habits
- Look for signs of learned helplessness, and re-engage
- Disrupting 'business as usual'
- People don't change if we don't lead it
- Leadership means leading change, not managing the status quo

Catapult Consulting

What will the future look like if you make no changes to your leadership:

Future by Design

Consider your personal future as a leader

Re-write your future by considering the following steps:

- Make a declaration!
- Create futures which inspire action
- Futures must speak to everyone in the process
- Describe a future as if it already exists in the moment of speaking
- Enrol every voice in the vision

Catapult Consulting

Now describe your future as a 21st century transformational leader:

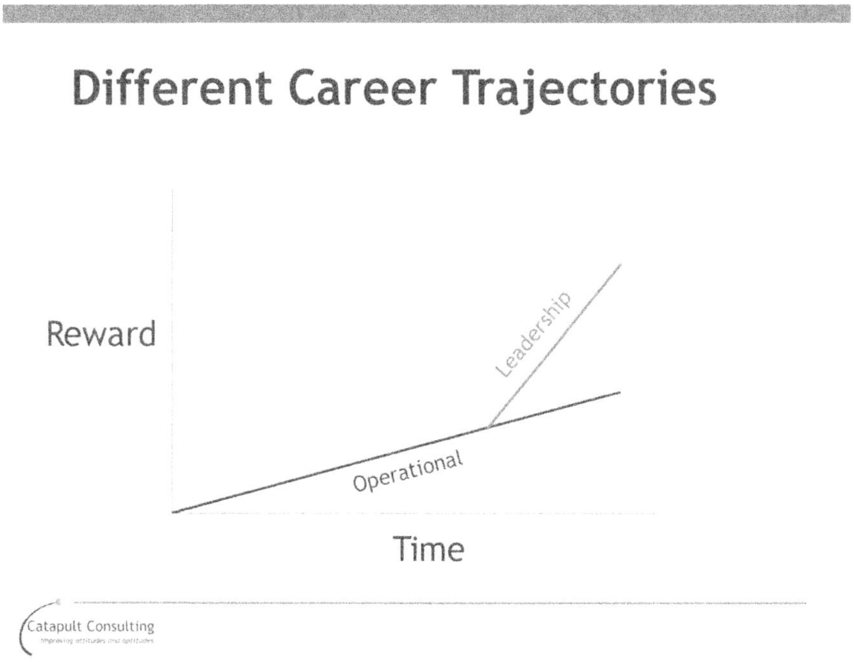

So, have you decided which path you are going to follow?

And are you truly ready for the weighty responsibility of leadership?

Leadership Manifesto

It's time to make your commitment to leadership!

Take a moment now to reflect on the learning and insights you have gleaned throughout this program and this workbook. How will you go about putting your learning to work?

Even if you don't yet have 'leader' in your job title or your job description, the brilliant thing about leadership is that you can lead from wherever you stand. Sometimes, the best leaders may be the people who weren't necessarily the most technically adept or operationally competent; maybe they are just really good at understanding and motivating people.

So, think carefully about the impact you want to create in the world, and the leadership legacy which will make you proud.

Here's an example of a leadership manifesto:

Leadership Manifesto

In order to build a high performance team, I develop a strong team identity, and provide tailored support to each member of my team, as required.

I lead my teams with transparency, setting clear expectations and a realistic psychological contract, sharing information about matters which affect them and giving feedback fairly, courageously and promptly. I ask for feedback from my teams, and if I forget, I always thank them for finding the time and making the effort to share it with me.

I believe that everyone is brilliant at something. I work to help people find authentic careers, to enjoy their work and to live to their highest potential. Failure of members of my team is failure of my leadership.

I always fight groupthink. I vow to push myself and my team to be the very best versions of ourselves. C. Sutherland, 12th April 2004

Catapult Consulting
Improving attitudes and aptitudes

Leadership Manifesto:

Your Personal Board of Directors

A mentor	______________________
A coach	______________________
An industry insider	______________________
A trendsetter	______________________
A connector	______________________
An idealist	______________________
A realist	______________________
A visionary	______________________
A partner	______________________
A mentee	______________________

Catapult Consulting

Take a moment to populate your personal board of directors with the names of people who can influence you to be a high-impact leader.

Don't worry if you don't actually know some of these people. As long as you can read about them, follow them on social media or find out more about them, you can take inspiration from them, and they can still serve on your personal board of directors.

Maintaining the Momentum

Things will only change if YOU change them.

Keep on keeping on...

- Communities of practice
- Best practice club
- Knowledge networks
- Reading and insights
- Shared folder
- Personal board of directors

Catapult Consulting
Improving attitudes and aptitudes

How will you stay on top of your game?

Routes to Learning & Development

Whenever we talk about learning and development, many people automatically think of formal training, but there are many ways to learn and develop, and formally taught courses forms only a small part of this. Learning at work can be achieved by:

70% 'Experience' - On the job learning

20% 'Exposure' - Guidance from someone else

10% 'Education' - Formal training courses

Below, there are some ideas of how you can direct the people in your teams to the various sources of learning and development available.

70%	20%	10%
• On the job experience • Job shadowing • Reading the process or the manual • New projects • Networking • Observation • Self directed learning • Reading • Researching best practice • e-Learning • Mentoring someone else on how to do it • Others? • •	• Working with more experienced people • Working with a coach • Working with a mentor • Networking • Implementing best practice approaches • Attending seminars • Conferences • Working groups • Reading a book or journal on the subject • TED talks and podcasts • Learning from someone else who has attended a course • Others? •	• Attending a training course run internally or externally • Others? •

As a leader, you need to invest in your own development, too.

Personal Growth and Development

Some leaders worry that giving too much praise or positive feedback sets the expectation of a pay rise or a promotion which may not be forthcoming, so they tend to dumb down their attempts at recognition. As we mentioned before, this can lead to a decline in performance and engagement and create more work for you in the long run.

Helping our high performers to maintain their levels of success requires some careful thought.

Thinking back to the SPACE analysis, what is important to each person in your team, with particular regard to their aspirations? How could you help them to get closer to realising those aspirations?

Think specifically along the following lines:

- Role expansion
- High profile projects
- Additional training and development to support their career ambitions
- A mentor or coach
- Job shadowing
- A lateral career move within the same company
- Time off to study or work towards a professional qualification
- Others?
-
-
-
-

If the person in your team really is a high performer, they may have their eye on your job. Don't worry - there will be plenty of opportunity for you slowly to hand over some of your responsibilities, gradually delegating more and more, which will make your life easier in the long run.

It will also free you up to make your next big move, too.

Other Leadership Development Ideas

Here are several other ideas you might consider when thinking about growing and developing your team... and yourself. Some are better suited to certain types of organization, and you may need to discuss with HR before you get started.

- **Book Club**

If the budget you have for training doesn't meet the needs and appetite of the team, consider doing a team book club. Allocate one professional text to each person on a subject which is personally and professionally relevant. Ask them to read it (give them a deadline), then to summarise the key learning points in a short presentation to the rest of the team. This is a great way to raise your level of knowledge and share ideas about business improvement and best practice.

- **Open Training**

If you are buying in a training course for your people, you could consider inviting people from other teams, or even other people within your professional network on a reciprocal basis. If your company invites people from their company to attend your training, they can offer people from your company the opportunity to attend training they have arranged, in return.

- **Set up a Knowledge Network**

This activity involves inviting people from across your professional network (in non-competing organizations) to meet up and discuss ideas and practices which have worked in their company, which might also work in yours. You could invite members of your team to be speakers at these events, which will help to cement their learning, and raise their professional profile. This activity works well if you arrange it for every couple of months. There is no cost (except maybe for coffee and biscuits), but you have to be invited to join the network.

- **Work Placements or Role Exchange**

Again, look to your professional network, and see if there is another comparable (but not competing) organization with a great reputation and high performance culture. You could consider arranging a work placement exchange with a high performer in your team and a high performer in theirs. Each employee swaps roles and desks for a prescribed period (maybe 3 - 6 months) in order to gain experience in another organization without running the risk of losing them to the competition. The cost for this is usually minimal - your employee stays on your payroll, and the employee from the organization stays on theirs.

Action speaks louder than words!

- What has been your biggest learning point from this text?
- What 3 actions will you take as a result of reading it?
- What will you never do again?
- Find someone to work with, who will hold you accountable

If not you, then who?
If not now, then when?

Catapult Consulting
Improving attitudes and aptitudes

What have been your big takeaways from this Blueprint for 21st Century Leadership workbook?

What do you want to discuss further, for example during conversations with your business coach?

What actions will you take to put your ideas into practice?

When will you take those actions?

Who will hold you accountable?

What obstacles can you anticipate which might prevent you from achieving your action plan?

What steps can you take right now to ensure that those obstacles don't prevent you from making the significant progress expected of you?

Personal Reflection

What have you learned about yourself as a future leader?

How you will integrate this learning to raise your leadership game?

Final Activity:

You are the leader:

Begin.

Catapult Consulting
Improving attitudes and aptitudes

CONCLUSION

Leadership is a privilege, shaping the futures of individuals, teams and organizations. You owe it to everyone concerned to do the best job possible.

Don't confuse management and leadership. Most roles involve a degree of both, but make sure you are focusing appropriately. Management is doing things right and leadership is doing the right things. Managers focus on the operational challenges, while leaders look to the future and inspire a compelling vision, enrolling everyone in delivering that vision.

People are fascinating, diverse, and trying their best. Lead by giving them what they want, not just by trying to bend them to your will. 'Command & Control' style of leadership works brilliantly in a crisis, but for the rest of the time, 'Convene and Discuss' is a much more democratic and collaborative way to lead others, and crucial when leading change and evolution.

Never quit learning - you always have time to be better, think smarter and get the best out of your people. Don't fall into complacency; always be hungry to know more.

Finally, the success of your people and of your organization is a reflection of the impact of your leadership. Good luck on your journey to becoming a 21st century leader.

Tools and Techniques

Here is a quick reminder of all the tools and techniques covered in this workbook, and when you can use them to greatest effect as you become a 21st century leader.

Tool	Clarifying the vision	Setting goals	Sustaining high performance	Communicating change	Influencing others
Myers Briggs		Y	Y	Y	
Strengths	Y	Y	Y	Y	Y
SPACE analysis		Y	Y	Y	Y
Generations	Y	Y	Y	Y	
Strengths CV		Y	Y	Y	Y
Coaching Questions		Y	Y	Y	Y
Skill / will		Y	Y	Y	
Goal alignment	Y	Y	Y	Y	Y
Change curve	Y	Y	Y	Y	Y
Cultural iceberg	Y	Y	Y	Y	
Leader or manager		Y	Y	Y	
Crucible conversations		Y	Y	Y	
Contextual leadership	Y	Y	Y		Y
Urgent & important	Y	Y	Y		Y
Motivation & engagement		Y	Y	Y	Y

Tool	Clarifying the vision	Setting goals	Sustaining high performance	Communicating change	Influencing others
Comms escalator	Y	Y		Y	Y
Stakeholder management	Y	Y	Y	Y	Y
Contextualise / localise	Y	Y	Y	Y	
PESTLE / SWOT analyses	Y	Y	Y	Y	
Microleadership	Y	Y	Y	Y	Y
Leadership styles	Y		Y	Y	Y
Servant leadership	Y	Y	Y	Y	Y
Accountability loop		Y	Y	Y	
Strategic framework	Y	Y	Y		
Conflict management			Y	Y	Y
Power styles		Y	Y	Y	Y
Agenda for 1:1 meeting					Y
VUCA / VUCA Prime	Y	Y	Y	Y	Y
Persuasion			Y	Y	Y
Leadership manifesto	Y	Y	Y	Y	Y

Further Reading

This Blueprint for 21st Century Leadership workbook will get you off to a flying start, but to enhance your knowledge and understanding of leading and inspiring for high performance, you might like to read some of the following texts:

Other Books by the Author

As a manager, setting goals and managing the performance of your people is YOUR job.

In this comprehensive workbook, you will find everything you need to know, including:

- Understanding motivation
- How to set meaningful goals with high commitment
- How to review progress towards goals
- The best questions for coaching individuals to success
- How to navigate a Crucible Conversation
- How to get reward and recognition right
- Building and sustaining a culture of high performance

Publisher Catapult Consulting Limited, 2022
ISBN 1739812905, 9781739812904
Length 106 pages

This workbook serves as a useful standalone text for staff who are new to management and keen to make the best possible start.

It is also the accompanying workbook to our 2-day "Management Masterclass" training program.

Drop us a line to find out more:

info@catapultconsulting.co.uk

Acknowledgements

To MG, my Editor-in-Chief: thank you for your extraordinary patience, critical eye and unremitting support for my endeavours.

Printed in Great Britain
by Amazon

44508669R00123